Our Walk in Christ

Exploring Practical Keys About the Journey of Life

Janet M. Magiera

LWM Publications

Versions quoted are noted by abbreviations after the verse citation as follows:

APNT: Aramaic Peshitta New Testament Translation, LWM Publications, 2006.

CJB: Complete Jewish Bible, David H. Stern, Jewish New Testament Publications, Inc., 1998.

ESV: English Standard Version, Crossway, a publishing ministry of Good News Publishers, 2001.

KJV: King James Version of the English Bible, 1769 Blayney edition.

Lamsa: The Holy Bible from Ancient Eastern Manuscripts, A.J. Holman Company, 1968.

MRD: The New Testament, A Literal Translation from the Syriac Peshito Version, 1851, public domain.

NASB: The New American Standard Version, The Lockman Foundation, 1977.

NET: The NET Bible, Biblical Studies Press, 1996.

NIV: New International Version, International Bible Society, 2011.

NLT: New Living Translation, Tyndale House Publishers, 1996.

TPT: The Passion Translation, Broadstreet Publishing Group, 2017.

LWM Publications is a division of:

Light of the Word Ministry
6213 Lake Athabaska Place
San Diego CA 92119
www.lightofword.org

ISBN No. 978-17326625-3-7

Copyright © 2021, Janet M. Magiera

Acknowledgements

This book is the culmination of a lot of different teachings that I have done over the years and because of that, I would like to acknowledge the support, encouragement and teaching opportunities afforded to me by various ministries and fellow ministers. Among these are Acts Now Fellowship, Victory in Christ Ministries, Muskegon Waves of Grace, Living in the Hope Ministry, Biblical Study Centers of Houston, The God Place, Christian Family Fellowship Ministry, Joint Heirs with Christ and Oakdale Bible Fellowship.

I could not have produced the book without the tremendous editing skills and advice of Trish Barbera. Suggestions and loving input were provided by Dan Connell and Sheila Hitchcock. I am grateful for the assistance of Cal Bower of One of a Kind Websites on the cover design.

I would like to thank the supporters and faithful contributors to Light of the Word Ministry, without which I could not have the time and leisure to devote to projects such as these.

And last but not least, I want to thank my dear husband and friend Glen who is always an extremely loyal supporter of all of my endeavors.

May God richly bless and pour out his mercy and grace on all of you. I'm thankful for being able to share this wonderful topic with you.

Table of Contents

Chapter 1 ❖ The Walk of our Life

Before we even start talking about walking on our journey of life, we have to realize that we need to sit before we walk. Think about children and how they learn to walk. They don't just get up and start walking. They learn to sit first and then they learn to crawl and then they stumble around for a while pulling themselves up, right?

There are several key concepts in Ephesians. The first one I want to look at is sitting together. "Sit together" could be translated "sit down together" or "be seated."

> *Ephesians 2:4-7 KJV*
> *4 But God, who is rich in mercy, for his great love wherewith he loved us,*
> *5 Even when we were dead in sins, hath quickened us together with Christ, (by grace ye are saved;)*
> *6 And hath raised us up together, and made us sit together in heavenly places in Christ Jesus:*
> *7 That in the ages to come he might shew the exceeding riches of his grace in his kindness toward us through Christ Jesus.*

There was a man named Watchman Nee who was an evangelist to China and he started his ministry around 1920. He traveled throughout all of China and he's one of the first evangelists who started underground churches in China. Today his pioneering work continues and we have no idea how many millions of people in China are born again, primarily because of his efforts and those he reached. In 1952, he ended up in prison for 20 years. Yet, in spite of the fact that he was unable to continue to travel, his work flourished.

He wrote a very famous book called *Sit, Walk, Stand*. It explains that the first three chapters of Ephesians are about who we are in Christ and where we are seated together with him. Then, from Ephesians 4:1-6:9, it is about walking according to who we are in Christ. Ephesians 6:10

and following are about standing. Here is an excerpt about sitting from Nee's book which I think sums up his premise very well.

> Let us first consider the implications of this word "sit." As we have said, it reveals the secret of a heavenly life. Christianity does not begin with walking; it begins with sitting. The Christian era began with Christ, of whom we are told that, when he made purification for sins, he "sat down on the right hand of the Majesty on high" (Hebrews 1:3). With equal truth, we can say that the individual Christian life begins with a man "in Christ"– that is to say, when by faith we see ourselves seated together with him in the heavenlies.
>
> Most Christians make the mistake of trying to walk in order to be able to sit, but that is a reversal of the true order. Our natural reason says, *If we do not walk, how are we ever going to get to the goal? What can we attain without effort? How can we ever get anywhere where we do not move?* But Christianity is a queer business! If at the outset we try to do anything, we get nothing; and if we seek to attain something, we miss everything. For Christianity begins not with the big DO, but with a big DONE. Thus Ephesians opens with the statement that God has "blessed us with every spiritual blessing in the heavenly places in Christ" (1:3) and we are invited at the very outset to sit down and enjoy what God has done for us; not to set out to try and attain it for ourselves.[1]

This book is about the walk of our lives as Christians, but I just wanted us to remember that even though we're going to be talking a lot about walking, Christianity begins with all that is done for us in Christ. If we ever get mixed up about walking, we should go back to the first three chapters of the book of Ephesians. When we read that we have been

---

[1] Watchman Nee, *Sit, Walk, Stand*, p. 2.

Chapter 1 ∵ The Walk of Our Life

blessed with all spiritual blessings, let's just stop there and sit down to rest. Then we can begin to think about walking again.

Walking is an interesting concept because in the Hebrew way of thinking, it simply means to live. Walking also includes physical walking, which we do all the time, even in our culture. Let's think about walking in general. I like to go walking at a lake near my house. Picture how in order to enjoy a walk there, I have to go get in my car. I sit in my car. I drive to the lake and then I park the car and then I might sit there for a little while. Then I get up and go on the path. And when I'm done walking then I go back and I sit in my car. There is no such thing as continual walking. There's always a process of resting in between walking and if one can do that, then he actually can walk a very long time and for a long distance.

It actually does not require a huge amount of physical strength to walk. If you are a dancer or gymnast or someone who plays sports, you need a highly developed set of muscles in order to do those kinds of things and be really good at them. While I'm not that good at any of those things, I am a good walker. Everyone can walk and that is why it is such a beautiful illustration.

Thayer's Greek Lexicon defines the Greek word *peripateo*, which is the word for to walk, as "to walk, walk about, to make one's way, progress, to make due use of opportunities. Hebraistically, to live, to regulate one's life."[2] Walking is a step-by-step process. And if you have a reasonable pace, you can walk continuously (with times of rest and sleep).

> *Ephesians 4:1 ESV*
> *I therefore, a prisoner for the Lord, urge you to walk in a manner worthy of the calling to which you have been called,*

---

[2] *Thayer's Greek Lexicon*, p. 564.

Chapter 1 ∵ The Walk of Our Life

The word "in a manner worthy of" in Greek is the word *axios*. Bullinger's Lexicon defines *axios* as "in a manner of equal value with the thing referred to."[3] The exhortation in this first verse of the practical side of Ephesians is to live out in practice what we have been called to as sons of God and joint-heirs with Christ. In addition, there are several other ways we are to walk worthily besides the calling. The first one is to walk as is becoming to the gospel of Christ. Our walk should have as much weight as the gospel of Christ.

> *Philippians 1:27 APNT*
> *Conduct yourselves as is becoming to the gospel of Christ, so that if I come, I may see you and if I am distant, I may hear about you, that you are standing in one spirit and in one soul and [that] you are conquering together in the faith of the gospel.*

We are also to walk in a manner worthy of the Lord and as is becoming to God. It is how we live out the matchless calling of God to his glory.

> *Colossians 1:10 ESV*
> *so as to walk in a manner worthy of the Lord, fully pleasing to him: bearing fruit in every good work and increasing in the knowledge of God;*

> *1 Thessalonians 2:12 APNT*
> *that you should walk as is becoming to God, who called you to his kingdom and to his glory.*

We get several words in English from the word *axios*, including axiom and axle. In his book, *In Heavenly Places*, Charles Welch explains that "Ephesians is the picture of a scale with a fulcrum and two sides that hold things. The one side is the calling and the other side is the walk. On the one scale all the blessings, the riches, the glories of our calling as revealed in Ephesians 1-3; on the other scale the walk that should

---

[3] Bullinger, *A Critical Lexicon and Concordance*, p. 904.

Chapter 1 ∴ The Walk of Our Life

balance these blessings, these riches, these glories, the walk that brings the beam of the balance to the horizontal, the walk that is "worthy of the calling."[4]

This first verse of Ephesians 4 is showing us that our lives need to be balanced between doctrine and practice. If either side is too heavy, then the scale will tip up or down. When we are talking about walking worthy of our calling, it means that we live our lives in balance based on who we are in Christ.

At any time, if either the doctrine or the practice is too heavy, then what is going to happen is that we're going to go in that direction and turn that way. I recall seeing that vividly with my granddaughter when she was learning to run. She was walking pretty straight, but when she tried to run, she didn't run in a straight line at first. Her body was following where she was looking and she was looking to the side. So she ended up running in a circle! That's what happens to us when we focus on one side to the detriment of the other (doctrine or practice).

If we relate this to physical walking, we can understand how crucial it is. If we walked with our bodies tipped far to the right or left, or even backward or forward, it would be very difficult to get anywhere. God designed the physical body to walk in an upright position, in balance.

The use of the term "to walk" to describe living and conducting ourselves is singularly apropos. If we look for a moment at what a physical, literal walk is not, it will be easy to see this. A walk is not a run. It is slower, steadier, and there is plenty of time to look around at the scenery. Compared to running, a walk does not require extreme exertion of energy. A walk is not a sprint. Sprinting means running full force but only for a limited time and distance. A person could walk steadily at a reasonable pace for as long as necessary. Anyone can be a great walker. Another contrast to note is that to walk does not mean to

---

[4] Charles Welch, *In Heavenly Places*, p. 327.

take a few steps and sit down. We are not to be "couch potatoes" where we sit most of the time and only walk a few steps. Walking implies movement. Also, a walk is not the broad jump or flying leaps of dancers. It can be slow or fast paced, but it is always one step at a time, one foot following the other.

The results of this balanced life are stated further in Colossians.

> *Colossians 1:10-11 KJV*
> *10 That ye might walk worthy of the Lord unto all pleasing, being fruitful in every good work, and increasing in the knowledge of God;*
> *11 Strengthened with all might, according to his glorious power, unto all patience and longsuffering with joyfulness;*

The results of a walk worthy of the Lord are: 1) fruitfulness in every good work, 2) increasing or abounding in the knowledge of God, 3) being strengthened with all might and 4) patience with joyfulness. To walk physically, even as doctors and health advisors say, is the best exercise where almost all areas of the body are strengthened and vitalized.

We will be learning a lot of different aspects about this walk or journey of our life, but let's remember that it is a balanced walk and we are to walk worthy of the calling we have in Christ Jesus.

Chapter 2 ❖ Walk – How?

There are a number of adverbs used in the New Testament that describe how we are to walk. The first one I want to look at is *euschemos*, meaning honestly or becomingly. Physically I think of walking gracefully, head held high, shoulders back. In life it means to conduct one's life with integrity and with grace. Integrity and honesty in all of our dealings in life are crucial to have good results. Gracefulness and ease in life come by living in and by God's grace. He made us lovely and acceptable in his sight (Ephesians 1:4). These two factors, integrity and grace, make our walk, our life, beautiful.

> *1 Thessalonians 4:12 KJV*
> *That ye may walk honestly [euschemos] toward them that are without, and that ye may have lack of nothing.*

That is a great promise for this life! If we walk honestly, we will have lack of nothing. It reminds me of many other promises in the Bible, such as Matthew 6:33, Philippians 4:19 and 2 Corinthians 9:8.

Another adjective, *akribos*, is used with "walk" in only one verse.

> *Ephesians 5:15-17 KJV*
> *15 See then that ye walk circumspectly, [akribos] not as fools, but as wise,*
> *16 Redeeming the time, because the days are evil.*
> *17 Wherefore be ye not unwise, but understanding what the will of the Lord is.*

Akribos means diligently, precisely, with perfect manner, accurately. It was used in Greek literature to describe how a person would climb to the top or summit of a mountain.[5] A related word is *akribestatos* used in Acts 26:5 where Paul described himself as living "after the most

---

[5] Bullinger, *A Critical Lexicon and Concordance*, p. 154.

straightest sect of our religion" as a Pharisee. How to walk circumspectly is spelled out in verses 16 and 17 in Ephesians 5. We need to redeem the time, take advantage of every opportunity to serve, to love, to care, by determining and understanding what the will of the Lord is. He will guide us in a precise manner even though we are in the middle of evil days.

Another word used with "walk" is the adverb, *ataktos*. This word means "disorderly, out of the ranks (often so of soldiers); irregular; deviating from the prescribed order or rule."[6] In 2 Thessalonians 3 it is used two times.

> *2 Thessalonians 3:6, 11-12 KJV*
> *6 Now we command you, brethren, in the name of our Lord Jesus Christ, that ye withdraw yourselves from every brother that walketh disorderly [ataktos], and not after the tradition which he received of us.*
> *11 For we hear that there are some which walk among you disorderly [ataktos], working not at all, but are busybodies.*
> *12 Now them that are such we command and exhort by our Lord Jesus Christ, that with quietness they work, and eat their own bread.*

The tradition that they received from Paul was not a certain method of work, but a lifestyle where he diligently and quietly worked to take care of his own physical needs. Walking "disorderly" is the opposite of that – to expect others to always take care of you and to be busybodies, meddling in other people's affairs. It says not to "hang out" with people who live like that. To say this positively, we should live our lives with quietness and we should take care of our own families. This reminds me of Titus 1:7-9 which is the passage that describes the qualifications of a bishop or elder. An elder should be "a lover of hospitality, a lover of good men, sober, just, holy, temperate; holding fast the faithful word as he hath been taught…"

---

[6] *Thayer's Greek Lexicon*, p. 83.

Chapter 2 ∴ Walk – How?

Another adverb used with "walk" is the word for acting uprightly, *orthopodeo*. It literally means to be "straight-footed." It is to walk in a straight line, not crookedly. We need to walk uprightly. If someone is bent over and tries to walk, it is very hard to go anywhere. First of all, if we are looking at the ground, we cannot see where we are going. We need to walk uprightly which basically just means straightly.

Orthopodeo is used in Galatians 2, when Peter went to Antioch and influenced other believers to go back to the Jewish customs.

> *Galatians 2:14 KJV*
> *But when I saw that they walked not uprightly [orthopodeo] according to the truth of the gospel, I said unto Peter before them all, If thou, being a Jew, livest after the manner of Gentiles, and not as do the Jews, why compellest thou the Gentiles to live as do the Jews?*

Truth is the straight line by which we walk. If we veer off the path and walk according to the traditions of men, we will not be "straight-footed." I believe this straight path has to do with not getting tricked by all the fronts of idolatry. Idolatry, not putting God first, is disguised by self, others, culture and religion. Anyone who looks at anything other than God and his Word will start to walk in that direction and end up stepping aside. That is what happened to Peter in Antioch and we can prevent it from happening to us when we walk on the straight path of truth.

Another way we walk is to pursue a path or journey. That Greek word is *poreuo*, "to pursue the journey on which one has entered."[7] It is used in Luke chapter 1 about Zacharias and Elizabeth.

> *Luke 1:6 ESV*
> *And they were both righteous before God, walking [poreuomai] blamelessly in all the commandments and statutes of the Lord.*

---

[7] *Thayer's Greek Lexicon*, p. 531.

Chapter 2 ∴ Walk – How?

It says both of them, both Zacharias, who was the priest, and Elizabeth, his wife, were just before God and were walking in all his commandments and in the uprightness (or righteousness) of the Lord without blame. The first thing that we see here is that they walked straightly and uprightly. The second thing is that they were walking in something; they were pursuing a journey. In this case, they were walking according to the commandments of the written Law, which is what they knew, and it says they were without blame. Now does that mean that they were perfect? Or that they never did anything wrong? No, it just means that they were righteous and so were blameless in the sight of God. We also need to walk according to or in something and we will learn more about that later.

Another adverb used with walking is to walk orderly. The Greek word is *stoicheo* and it means "to proceed in a row, go in order."[8] Its first use is in Acts 21, when Paul was going to Jerusalem and he had made a vow.

> *Acts 21:24 KJV*
> *Them take, and purify thyself with them, and be at charges with them, that they may shave their heads: and all may know that those things, whereof they were informed concerning thee, are nothing; but that thou thyself also walkest orderly [stoicheo], and keepest the law.*

Paul was walking orderly according to what was necessary to do to keep this vow that he had made and to pay the expense for it. The word "orderly" is actually a military term about a soldier who is learning to march and walk in a file. The soldiers would line up in a file and then fall in line and march step by step. I saw that when my son Mark first graduated from the Marine Corps. He learned how to march in formation and according to the direction of the commander. They had a grand demonstration of this at the graduation ceremony. Thus, to walk orderly is first to walk in a row, step by step.

---

[8] *Thayer's Greek Lexicon*, p. 589.

Chapter 2 ∴ Walk – How?

Romans 4:12 APNT
and the father to the circumcision, not to those who are from the
circumcision only, but also to those who follow in the footsteps of the
faith of the uncircumcision of our father Abraham.

"Follow" is the Aramaic idiom, literally translated, "to go after" and compares to *stoicheo*. It is talking about walking in literal footsteps or tracks. We are to follow in the footsteps of the faith of Abraham. How? He was in uncircumcision when he was in Ur of the Chaldees and there, God first called him and first gave him a promise. God told him to go to a country that he would show him. Abraham didn't hesitate. He just started walking. Did he really know where he was going? He had never been there before, but as he walked God showed him what the next steps were. And that is why Abraham is our example of faith.

These descriptions of how to walk paint a beautifully complete picture of the kind of conduct we should have in our everyday life. We are to keep in balance, not emphasizing doctrine more than practice. We are to live with honesty and integrity and thus will have lack of nothing. We are to walk with accuracy and precision, discerning what the will of the Lord is. We are to live in quietness, working to take care of our own affairs. We are to walk straight-footed on the truth of the gospel, pursuing our journey and we are to walk in an orderly manner. The walk of the Word is like physical walking, keeping upright, head and shoulders back, one precise step at a time on a straight path.

Chapter 3 ❖ Where is the Path?

One of the biggest questions that believers have all over the world, no matter where they are, is where is the path? Where is my path? Where am I supposed to be walking? This chapter will cover some points about how to find the path and where it is.

> *Proverbs 4:25-27 ESV*
> *25 Let your eyes look directly forward, and your gaze be straight before you.*
> *26 Ponder the path of your feet; then all your ways will be sure.*
> *27 Do not swerve to the right or to the left; turn your foot away from evil.*

Verse 25 has the same idea as in the last chapter about looking straight ahead and walking straightly. And verse 27 reiterates the idea that our walk should be balanced, not to the right or left, or too heavy on doctrine or practice. But notice the promise in verse 26 that if we ponder the path of our feet, all our ways will be sure or established. This verse could be literally translated, "make level the goings of your feet and all your paths will be established." In other words, take all the obstacles out of the way of walking in God's path for you.

I actually believed for a long time that it was very hard to find the path. I got this idea from a passage in Matthew.

> *Matthew 7:13-14 NASB*
> *13 Enter through the narrow gate; for the gate is wide and the way is broad that leads to destruction, and there are many who enter through it.*
> *14 For the gate is narrow and the way is constricted that leads to life, and there are few who find it.*

The door is narrow and the road is constricted that leads to life because it is only by believing on the Lord Jesus Christ that we have access to salvation. But once we go through the door or gate, the path becomes very wide and there are beautiful green pastures. The wide door or gate is easy to go in and the road in is broad, but then the path becomes crooked and leads to destruction. Jesus said he was the gate or the door.

> *John 10:7-9 APNT*
> *7 Now again Jesus said to them, "Truly, truly I say to you, I am the gate of the flock.*
> *8 And all those who come are thieves and robbers, unless the flock hears them.*
> *9 I am the gate and if anyone should enter by me, he will live. And he will enter and he will go out and find pasture."*

The door is narrow, but the path is wide once you get through the door and you start walking on the path. What God really wants is for us to have a relationship with him right now and to walk as sons of God with power; that takes going into the pasture. That's why once you get through the door, there is a beautiful wide pasture to walk in. It is not difficult to walk on the path then. There are a number of verses that talk about this wide path.

> *Psalm 119:45 ESV*
> *and I shall walk in a wide place, for I have sought your precepts.*

There is so much freedom and so much liberty in this wide place that every single person in the body of Christ has a place to walk.

> *Psalm 18:32-36 ESV*
> *32 the God who equipped me with strength and made my way blameless.*
> *33 He made my feet like the feet of a deer and set me secure on the heights.*
> *34 He trains my hands for war, so that my arms can bend a bow of bronze.*

Chapter 3 ∴ Where is the Path?

35 You have given me the shield of your salvation, and your right hand supported me, and your gentleness made me great.
36 You gave a wide place for my steps under me, and my feet did not slip.

There is a wide place for our steps, so that they do not slip. The illustration of the deer emphasizes his agility. The deer can scamper up a mountain swiftly and find a spot at the top of the mountain where he can see if there is an enemy or foe coming. He can also look down and clearly see the path. There is a wide path, but it is also "on the heights."

The path is a level place, too.

> *Psalm 26:11-12 ESV*
> *11 But as for me, I shall walk in my integrity; redeem me, and be gracious to me.*
> *12 My foot stands on level ground; in the great assembly I will bless the LORD.*

Somehow, we also get the picture that the climb up the mountain is lonely and we are like one small deer all alone on the top of that mountain trying to see the enemy. This is not just <u>my</u> path. This is all of our paths and we're all doing it together "in the great assembly." I am with all my brothers and sisters in this wide place that is level where we can see the enemy coming and we can help each other.

> *Psalm 27:11 ESV*
> *Teach me your way, O LORD, and lead me on a level path because of my enemies.*

God wants us to go into this wide place and to learn how to walk with him because there are a lot of enemies and also a lot of distractions to try to get us to go off of the path and turn to the right or to the left. But if we are walking on the path together and we are seeing it from the

Chapter 3 ∴ Where is the Path?

mountain top, that is a completely different position than just trying to weave your way alone through a narrow, crooked path.

> *Psalm 143:8-10 ESV*
> *8 Let me hear in the morning of your steadfast love, for in you I trust. Make me know the way I should go, for to you I lift up my soul.*
> *9 Deliver me from my enemies, O LORD! I have fled to you for refuge.*
> *10 Teach me to do your will, for you are my God! Let your good Spirit lead me on level ground!*

David's prayer was, "Let your good Spirit lead me on level ground." This path is worth talking about! It is wide and high and level. We have the full measure of the Spirit that Jesus Christ had and it is all we will ever need. By walking by that Spirit, we will know where to walk.

> *Philippians 2:14-16 APNT*
> *14 Do everything without murmuring and without division,*
> *15 so that you will be innocent and without blemish, as pure sons of God who are living in a perverted and crooked generation. And be seen among them as lights in the world,*
> *16 so that you will be to them in place of life, for my glory in the day of Christ, so that I have not run at random nor worked hard fruitlessly.*

Does it say that the path is crooked? It says that the generation we are living in is crooked. When we are tempted to get off this wide, level, high path that God has provided for us, we conform to the world and start walking according to their crooked, narrow, stingy path. We need to stay on the high ground, so to speak. Then we will be seen among them as lights in the world and we will be to them in place of life. We should allow the light to shine in our lives to reflect Christ to those people who want to know. We don't need to talk about what the crooked path is. All we have to be talking about is the gospel, which is that we can walk in this freedom, we can walk by the Spirit, and God will show us what we're supposed to do.

21

Chapter 3 ∴ Where is the Path?

This brings up a question that many believers have. Don't we live in the world and have to deal with the things of the world? The answer is yes, but no. We live on the mountaintop and beckon people from the world to join us in the wide, high, level pasture. We live our lives from the perspective of the heavenlies.

At the end of Galatians, it spells out that we are to walk according to the new creation. We look back at the crucifixion to see what our Lord accomplished for us, but then we follow or go after the path.

> *Galatians 6:14-16 APNT*
> *14 But [as] for me, I will have nothing to boast about except the cross of our Lord Jesus Christ, by whom the world is crucified to me and I am crucified to the world.*
> *15 For neither circumcision is anything, nor uncircumcision, but a new creation.*
> *16 And those who follow this path, peace and mercies will be on them and on the Israel of God.*

We are united together in this path, about which we will see more in the future chapters. We have so many examples to emulate of great men and women of God who have gone before us. In our day and time, we also have so many wonderful teachers and ministers to follow as examples.

> *Philippians 3:16-20 APNT*
> *16 Nevertheless, to reach this, we should follow in one path and with one agreement.*
> *17 Imitate me, my brothers, and consider those who so walk as an example that you have seen in us.*
> *18 For there are many who walk otherwise, those whom I have told you about many times, and now weeping, I am saying that they are enemies of the cross of Christ,*

Chapter 3 ∵ Where is the Path?

*19 whose end is destruction, whose god [is] their stomach and whose
glory [is] their shame, whose thinking is on the earth.
20 But our work is in heaven and from there we are expecting the
Savior, our Lord Jesus Christ,*

Our work, our citizenship is in heaven (on top of the mountain) and
from there we look to the Hope of Christ's return. The Passion
Translation shares verse 20 as, "But we are a colony of heaven on earth
as we cling tightly to our life-giver, the Lord Jesus Christ." Let's change
our picture of the "narrow gate" and step out to walk onto the wide,
level and high path that God has made available for us in Christ Jesus and
shine as lights to the world.

Chapter 4 ❖ Walk as Sons of Light

Another lie that the world tries to teach us is that the path is dark. When we walk on God's path, we are on a path of light. And "God is light, and in him is no darkness at all" (1 John 1:5).

> *Ephesians 5:8 APNT*
> *for you were first of all [in] darkness, but now you are light in our Lord. Therefore, so walk as sons of light,*

As we all at one time were in darkness, now there is light in us. As children of light, we can now have a change in our conduct. We were rescued from the kingdom of darkness and now can walk in the kingdom of God's beloved Son.

> *Colossians 1:12-13 APNT*
> *12 you should give thanks to God the Father, who has made us worthy for a portion of the inheritance of the holy [ones] in light*
> *13 and has delivered us from the authority of darkness and has transferred us to the kingdom of his beloved Son,*

When we walk in the light, it exposes the darkness. We don't go down to walk on the crooked path and try to shine our light. We shine the light at the top of the mountain and people see it and want to know where the path is to get there, too. We walk on the wide, high, level path and others will want to join us. Let's go back to Ephesians.

> *Ephesians 5:9-10 APNT*
> *9 for the effects of the light are in all goodness and justification and truthfulness.*
> *10 And determine what is pleasing before our Lord*

Light causes things to grow. It has a positive effect on everything around it. The first effect of the light is goodness or kindness of heart, a predisposition to do what is helpful to others. The second effect is that

Chapter 4 ∴ Walk as Sons of Light

God's righteousness is brought forth. The third effect is truthfulness or integrity. Integrity is something that is mighty hard to find in our day and time.

Verse 10 summarizes the point. A life "at home" in the light seeks what pleases God. It is like a plant growing towards the light in a window. Periodically you have to turn it around so the other side can seek the light. The light causes it to bloom and grow.

> *Ephesians 5:11-13 APNT*
> *11 and do not fellowship with the works of darkness that have no [good] effects, but reprove them,*
> *12 for what they do in secret is abominable even to speak,*
> *13 for everything is exposed and is revealed by the light and everything that reveals is light.*

In order to understand this section, we need to consider what was going on in Ephesus and why this passage was so apropos to the Ephesians. Ephesus was a very prosperous city in Asia Minor with a large harbor. In it was a temple to Diana or Artemis as she is also called. This was one of the seven wonders of the ancient world. It was 377 feet long and 151 feet wide, made of pure marble with 127 columns.[9] As Acts 19:35 describes, the people believed that her image had come down from heaven. The idol was a fertility goddess with many breasts and the people in Ephesus practiced many different kinds of curious arts and magic spells in her worship.

Ephesus was also a center of commercialism and trade. Silversmiths made shrines to Diana and people came from all over to worship and lie with the prostitutes in the temple. No one could be convicted of a crime within a bow shot of the temple, so the temple was surrounded by criminals.

---

[9] https://www.israeljerusalem.com/temple-of-diana-ephesus.htm

Chapter 4 ∴ Walk as Sons of Light

When Paul was in Ephesus many people believed the gospel and confessed their crimes. They burned their books, valued at five thousand pieces of silver, which is approximately five million dollars in our day.

Acts 19:18-20 APNT
18 And many of those who believed came and declared their faults and confessed what they had done.
19 And many sorcerers also gathered their books and brought [and] burned them before everyone. And they counted their price and the silver amounted to five thousand [pieces].
20 And so with great power the faith of God grew strong and increased.

During this time, there was a great riot that happened throughout the city, stirred up by one of the silversmiths, Demetrius.

Acts 19:23-28 APNT
23 And during that time a great uproar occurred about the way of God.
24 And there was there a certain worker of silver, whose name was Demetrius who was making shrines of silver for Artemis and he brought great profit to his fellow craftsmen.
25 This [man] gathered all his fellow craftsmen and those who worked with them and said to them, "Men, you know that all our trade is from this occupation.
26 And you have also heard and you have seen that this Paul has persuaded and turned away, not only the citizens of Ephesus, but also a multitude of all of Asia, saying that those are not gods that are made by the hands of men.
27 And not only this business is being shamed and brought to nothing, but also the temple of the great goddess Artemis is counted as nothing, and also the goddess, whom all Asia and all the Gentiles worship, is despised."
28 And when they heard these [things], they were filled with fury and cried out and said, "Great is Artemis of the Ephesians."

Chapter 4 ∴ Walk as Sons of Light

Eventually the riot was dispersed, but not until after the whole city had been affected.

We can see now that the passage in Ephesians was describing some pretty dark things. The light of the gospel came and reproved and exposed the darkness. Light is powerful without even trying. It exposes darkness by its very nature. That is why we need to walk in the light. It is actually part of our armor. We need to wake up and walk in the light!

> *Romans 13:11-14 APNT*
> *11 And also know this, that it is the time and the hour that from now on we should be awakened from our sleep. For now our life has come nearer to us than when we believed.*
> *12 Then the night is passed and the day is near. So we should lay aside from us the works of darkness and we should put on the armor of light.*
> *13 And we should walk in [this] manner, as in the day, not in reveling and not in drunkenness and not in a defiled bed and not in envy and in strife.*
> *14 But put on our Lord Jesus Christ and do not have regard for the desires that are in your flesh.*

Light is also reflective. People see us shining as I described in the last chapter. We shine out the light within and it shines on others. The purpose of this shining is to glorify God.

> *Matthew 5:14-16 APNT*
> *14 You are the light of the world. It is not possible to hide a city that is built on a mountain.*
> *15 And they do not light a lamp and place it under a basket, but on a lampstand and it lights all those who are in the house.*
> *16 Likewise, your light should shine before men, so that they will see your good works and will glorify your Father who is in heaven.*

Chapter 4 ∴ Walk as Sons of Light

Here are a few other verses about walking in the light to hold in our hearts.

> *John 8:12 APNT*
> *Now again Jesus spoke to them and said, "I am the light of the world. He who follows me will not walk in darkness, but he will find for himself the light of life."*

> *John 11:9-10 APNT*
> *9 Jesus said to them, "Are [there] not twelve hours in a day? And if a man walks in the day he will not stumble, because he sees the light of this world.*
> *10 But if a man should walk in the night, he will stumble, because he has no illumination."*

> *John 12:35-36 APNT*
> *35 Jesus said to them, "The light is with you [a little while] longer. Walk while you have light, so that the darkness will not overtake you. And he who walks in darkness does not know to where he goes.*
> *36 While you have the light, believe in the light that you may become sons of light." Jesus spoke these [things] and went [and] hid from them.*

Now we have Christ in us, so we can walk as sons of light all the time. To walk as sons of light then is to produce positive effects and see things grow, make visible the darkness and to shine on others so that God is glorified for he is the Light.

> *Proverbs 4:18 ESV*
> *But the path of the righteous is like the light of dawn, which shines brighter and brighter until full day.*

Chapter 5 ❖ Walking with What?

We have seen that we need to walk in balance, and in this chapter, we will explore how to do that and with what kinds of qualities. There are three qualities that we should walk "with."

> *Ephesians 4:1-2a APNT*
> *1 I, therefore, a prisoner in our Lord, beg you that you should walk as is proper for the calling that you were called,*
> *2 with all humbleness of mind and quietness and long-suffering....*

The first quality is humbleness of mind or meekness. We will first look at the Greek and then the Aramaic meanings of these words. The Greek word for humbleness is *tapeinophrosune*. Humility is a consistent theme throughout the epistles. In the Greco-Roman world many regarded humility as a sign of weakness or even a character flaw; its meanings of "lowly" or "servile" were often used disparagingly. That is true in our culture, too. That meekness should be the first quality in how to walk worthily is therefore quite striking. Paul writes that humility is at the heart of Christ's character.

> *Philippians 2:3-5 APNT*
> *3 And do not do anything with controversy or with empty boasting, but with humbleness of mind. Everyone should count his associate as better than himself.*
> *4 And a man should not be concerned for himself [only], but each one [should] also [be concerned] for his associate.*
> *5 And think this in yourselves which Jesus Christ also [thought],*

What is the definition of humbleness? Thayer defines the Greek word as "having a humble opinion of one's self; a deep sense of one's (moral) littleness."[10] This definition reminds me of the false religious idea that one should have a demeaning opinion of oneself. Most of the definitions

---

[10] *Thayer's Greek Lexicon*, p. 614.

have this connotation, so clearly, the word "humbleness" is one which needs to be understood in light of its Biblical usage.

> *1 Peter 5:5-6 APNT*
> *5 And you, young ones, be subject to your elders and be clothed diligently with humbleness of mind toward one another, because God is opposed to those who elevate themselves, but he gives grace to the humble.*
> *6 Therefore, humble yourselves under the mighty hand of God, so that he will elevate you in the time that is right.*

From these verses it is apparent that humbleness of mind is something a believer can put on, or that is cultivated in a person's life. It is a quality which God rewards with grace to those who do put it on (the humble) and resists those who do not (the proud).

So what does it mean to be humble? Many times, it is easier to understand the meaning of a word by looking at its verb root. The physical sense helps to make clearer the abstract concept. This is especially true in the Aramaic language, where often an abstract concept has a root verb that is either a physical action or picture. This is true with the Aramaic root verb of this word "humble." It is the Aramaic word *mak* and means "to lie down flat, prostrate oneself,"[11] or in other words, to lie down under.

What are we to lie down under? 1 Peter 5:6 explains that we are to lie down under the "mighty hand of God." This begins to tell us how to be meek. Jesus Christ is the perfect example of this characteristic.

> *Philippians 2:8 KJV*
> *And being found in fashion as a man, he humbled himself, and became obedient unto death, even the death of the cross.*

---

[11] J. Payne Smith, *A Compendious Syriac Dictionary*, p. 270.

Chapter 5 ∴ Walking with What?

Jesus Christ was completely obedient to God's will, even to his death. He subjected his own will to the will of God. In everything he saw himself as subject to God's purposes – his will, his love, his direction and guidance, his word.

> *James 1:21b APNT*
> *...and receive with meekness the word that is implanted in our nature that is able to give life to your souls.*

Makikutha is the Aramaic noun derived from *mak* and means meekness or humility. In this verse, we are to lie down under the Word of God.

In Matthew 11:29 Jesus Christ is called "meek and lowly." He always put his own will under the will of the Father. This is the first quality in our lives that we need to have in order to walk worthy of our calling.

> *Matthew 11:29-30 APNT*
> *29 Bear my yoke on you and learn from me that I am restful and I am meek in my heart, and you will find rest for your souls.*
> *30 For my yoke is pleasant and my burden is light.*

The Aramaic Peshitta has "restful" first and then "meek." We already know what meekness is, now what does restful mean and how to we find rest for our souls? This is the second quality from Ephesians 4:2 that we need to have – restfulness or quietness. The Greek word is *praotes*, which basically means mildness or gentleness. I don't think this is clear enough to understand the difference between meekness and restfulness. So let's look at the Aramaic.

The Aramaic word is *nakh*. The family of Aramaic words that belong to *nakh* is very interesting and helps to explain how to be quiet. There is a play on words in Matthew 11 with the words, "I will give you rest" [*nakh*], I am "restful" [*nakh*], and "you will find rest" [*neyakha*].

Chapter 5 ∴ Walking with What?

The Aramaic word *nakh* means "to rest, be at rest, stay quiet, to cease, be stayed."[12] The verb in its simplest form is used in Luke 8:24 where the wind and raging of the storm "ceased." The words derived from this verb all have to do with rest, quiet and cessation from something opposite (like the storm). When used regarding a ship, it could be translated "unload." We see that in order to have rest, we need to stop something or unload something.

Hebrews chapters 3 and 4 have eight uses of the noun *neyakhtha* and three uses of *nakh*, which indicate there would be keys there about this rest and how it could be obtained.

The context of Hebrews 3 and 4 is about the hardness of heart of Israel that was caused by their unbelief. Israel's behavior in the wilderness is given as an example of what not to do today. Those of Israel in the wilderness who had hardened their hearts did not enter into the rest of the Promised Land.

> *Hebrews 3:18-19 APNT*
> *18 And about whom did he swear that they would not enter into his rest [neyakththa], but about those who were not persuaded?*
> *19 We see that they were not able to enter, because they did not believe.*

Chapter 4 begins with an exhortation to do the opposite, that is to believe to be able to enter into rest.

> *Hebrews 4:3a APNT*
> *But we who believe are entering into rest [neyakhtha].*

Continuing on in Hebrews 4, the example is given how God rested on the seventh day from all his works. Just as God sat and rested after he had finished the works in Genesis 1 and 2, Christ also sat down at God's right hand (Ephesians 1:20) when our salvation and redemption was

---

[12] J. Payne Smith, *A Compendious Syriac Dictionary*, p. 331.

complete. The works for our complete wholeness have already been accomplished. Therefore, we have a right to rest.

> *Hebrews 4:10 APNT*
> *For he who enters into his rest [neyakhtha] has also rested [nakh] from his works, as God [rested] from his.*

Applied to us today, believers need to cease from their own works or unload their own ideas about works and instead literally believe the finished work of Christ. This will yield rest.

The Aramaic word in Hebrews 4:10 for "rested" is *nakh* again, this time in its Aphel, or intensified form. It means to cause to cease, put to rest, stop, put off. It is used in other verses about "putting off" the old man. To cease from our own works is to put off the old man. It means to stop, put to rest, cause to cease our own ideas of works. Hebrews 4:11 goes on to exhort us to be diligent.

> *Hebrews 4:11 APNT*
> *Therefore, we should be diligent to enter into that rest, so that we will not fall in the likeness of those who were not persuaded.*

This at first seems to be a contradiction – cease from works, but let us labour (as in the King James Version). To labour means to be diligent. Our diligence is to be in believing. Believing what? What God already made unto us in Christ Jesus. Thus, in these chapters of Hebrews, diligent believing of the accomplished work of Christ, rather than our own works, is the key to obtaining rest. Being restful is the result of lining up our believing with the Word of God.

There are three times when meekness and quietness are used together. They show the relationship with each other and give more practical keys on how to be restful and meek as Jesus Christ was and to walk like he did.

Chapter 5 ∴ Walking with What?

The first place is in 2 Corinthians 10:1 where Jesus Christ is again upheld as the example of both qualities. "Now I, Paul, beg you by the quietness and by the meekness of Christ…" (APNT). Paul is beseeching us here not to war after the flesh. How?

> *2 Corinthians 10:4-5 APNT*
> *4 For the equipment of our service is not of the flesh, but of the power of God and by it, we overcome rebellious strongholds.*
> *5 And we pull down reasonings and all pride that elevates [itself] against the knowledge of God and we lead captive all thoughts to the obedience of Christ.*

The first half of verse 5 agrees with all that has been seen in Hebrews. We must "cast down imaginations" or sense-knowledge reasonings, or "cease from our own works" or "put off the old man." We need to do this thought by thought, leading every thought captive to the obedience of Christ. True humility is to obey God's Word. The diligence to believe is in capturing each individual thought and then lining it up with the Word of God. What we are to believe is what God has already accomplished in Christ Jesus.

A simple example is when our heart begins to condemn ourselves for something we did wrong. We know that God has forgiven us in Christ Jesus, but the thought still remains that we are condemned. That is where a verse such as Romans 8:1 must replace the thoughts in our mind: "There is therefore now no condemnation for those who are in Christ Jesus" (NET).

Meekness and quietness are also used together in Colossians.

> *Colossians 3:12 APNT*
> *Therefore, as the chosen [ones] of God, holy and beloved, put on mercies and loving-kindness and gentleness and humbleness of mind and quietness and long-suffering.*

Chapter 5 ∴ Walking with What?

When we literally believe and are obedient to put on God's Word thought by thought, meekness becomes a foundational way of living that yields a gentle quietness. This quietness is an inward quality of restfulness and cessation of our own agenda and purposes. According to Vine's, "The common assumption is that when a man is meek it is because he cannot help himself; but the Lord was 'meek' because he had the infinite resources of God at His command. Described negatively, meekness is the opposite to self-assertiveness and self-interest: it is equanimity (evenness) of spirit that is neither elated nor cast down, simply because it is not occupied with self at all."[13]

With this study and understanding of these two words, one can now explore all the other uses of meekness and apply the principles to one's life. God's Word sets out clearly and simply the truth about these concepts which totally contradicts the world's viewpoint of meekness and quietness. Also, Jesus Christ's life can be studied to see these qualities and how they were manifested.

In Colossians, a third quality is listed that is also in Ephesians 4:2: long-suffering. That is also a word that does not sound very good to our ears and suffering doesn't sound good at all!

The Greek and Aramaic words are actually very similar. They both mean to lengthen out the time for emotions to take over. The Greek word *makrothumia* according to Thayer's Lexicon means, "to be of a long spirit, not to lose heart; hence, to be patient in bearing the offences and injuries of others; to be mild and slow in avenging; to be long-suffering, slow to anger, slow to punish."[14] It is a compound word made up of *makros* (long) and *thumia* (wrath). It means literally to go for a long period of time before exercising wrath.

---

[13] *Vine's Expository Dictionary*, p. 56.
[14] *Thayer's Greek Lexicon*, p. 387.

Chapter 5 ∴ Walking with What?

The Aramaic word is an idiom of two words, *negar* and *rukha*. The word *rukha* is the word for spirit or breath. This idiom is literally, to pour out the breath. *Negar* also has the idea of extending the time, or something going on for a long time. We use another idiom that has the same idea when something is going on: "take a deep breath." Longsuffering is pouring out time for things to work out.

The first characteristic of love is longsuffering (1 Corinthians 13:4) and we are to walk worthy of our calling with longsuffering. It is also a fruit of the spirit (Galatians 5:22). Let's look at a few verses that help us to understand the definitions.

> *1 Thessalonians 5:14 APNT*
> *Now we beg you, my brothers, instruct the wrong-doers and encourage the faint-hearted [ones] and bear the burden of weak [ones] and be long-suffering to everyone.*

This exhortation is to be longsuffering to everyone. This would mean it is possible to cultivate this quality with believers and unbelievers alike. This seems like a difficult task, but when we apply the action of pouring out the breath to the next verses, we will begin to see how to have longsuffering.

> *2 Timothy 2:23-24 APNT*
> *23 Avoid foolish controversies [with] those who are without instruction, for you know that they generate disputes.*
> *24 Now a servant of our Lord should not dispute, but he should be meek to everyone and adept at teaching and long-suffering.*

The opposite of longsuffering is to dispute, and the result of pausing, pouring out the breath, is to quell the dispute. Every time there is a potential dispute or argument, this quality becomes necessary.

An example of how to be longsuffering is in James about a farmer.

Chapter 5 ∴ Walking with What?

> *James 5:7 APNT*
> *But you, my brothers, be long-suffering until the coming of the LORD,*
> *as the farmer who waits for the precious fruit of his ground and is long-*
> *suffering about it, until he receives the early and latter rain.*

The farmer knows that with time (pouring out the breath) the rains will come at the appropriate time to cause the harvest to mature. If someone went to look for figs when they were not ripe and was angry about that, we would think he was pretty crazy. That is why this particular verb is often used with time.

> *James 5:8 APNT*
> *So also be long-suffering and establish your hearts, for the coming of*
> *our Lord draws close.*

To establish your hearts is to make them firm. Longsuffering takes resolve, but it is not difficult when we pause, pour out the breath, and then go on. In the Old Testament, the Hebrew word *nagar* is often translated "slow to anger." In fact, God is used as the primary example of longsuffering (Exodus 34:6).

> *1 Peter 3:20 APNT*
> *Those who previously were disobedient in the days of Noah, when [in]*
> *the long-suffering of God he commanded an ark to be made, in hope of*
> *their repentance, yet only eight souls entered it and were kept alive on*
> *the water.*

After God told Noah to build the ark, he waited for approximately one hundred years in hope of someone else repenting and being able to be saved. During that time Noah is called a preacher of righteousness (2 Peter 2:5) and certainly also exhibited the characteristic of longsuffering in light of the complete rejection of God from everyone around him. Pour out the breath and then go on. There is a distinct element of time with longsuffering.

Chapter 5 ∴ Walking with What?

Abraham is also used as an example of longsuffering. He received his son, Isaac, about 25 years after God gave the promise to him and after a series of lessons. He was "fully persuaded" (Romans 4:21) that what God had promised he was able to bring to pass. We can meditate on this in terms of our obtaining God's promises.

> *Hebrews 6:14-15 APNT*
> *14 And said: I will certainly bless you and I will greatly multiply you.*
> *15 And so he was long-suffering and received the promise.*

There is one verse in Romans about longsuffering, which summarizes these qualities we have been exploring.

> *Romans 3:26 APNT*
> *[It is] by the advantage that God in his long-suffering gave to us for the clear showing of his uprightness that is at this time, that he would be upright and would justify with uprightness him who is in the faith of our Lord Jesus Christ.*

God gave us the advantage of time by his longsuffering and he waited until we would believe. His desire for our repentance was so great that he "poured out his breath" in anticipation of us believing, so he could then pardon our sins. What a loving God! Then he justified us and declared us righteous as well. How could we do any less with our brothers and sisters especially, and with all men?

To walk worthy of our calling, we need to accompany our walk with these three qualities: meekness, quietness and long suffering. When we lie down under the Word of God and realize our salvation in Christ, we can be restful and quiet with that assurance and then extend time and love toward our brothers and sisters as well as ourselves. Remember, walking is a step-by-step process and we do not stop walking until Christ's return or our demise. So, pour out the breath and be an imitator of our Father, who extends mercy and grace unendingly.

Chapter 6 ❖ Forbearing One Another in Love

At the end of Ephesians 4:2 and also in verse 3, there are two participles that we will study in this chapter and the next. When you see a participle, especially if it is active, it shows that there needs to be some action associated with it. The first participle is "forbearing" or "holding."

> *Ephesians 4:2 MRD*
> *with all lowliness of mind, and quietness, and long suffering; and that ye be forbearing one towards another, in love.*

I chose this translation of the Aramaic because Murdock translates this clearly as a participle.

The word for forbearing in Aramaic is built on a special form of the verb, *sevar*. The simple meaning of *sevar* is to think, to consider, thus to hope or to wait. This particular form of the word is the Paiel tense which means it has an extra letter "yoth" in the middle of it. That adds the idea of power to "thinking and hoping" and then means to sustain, hold up, bear, forbear and sometimes suffer.[15] The overall sense is to endure. The picture for that particular tense is to hold up or to hold onto but it is linked to the simple meaning – to hope. We will see this further as we examine some of the verses where both the verb and noun are used.

> *1 Peter 2:20 APNT*
> *But what praise will they have who endure [sevar] pressures because of their transgressions? But when you do what is good and they pressure you and you endure [sevar], then your praise is great with God.*

I think this is the best verse that summarizes the heart of what forbearance is, that it means to endure. Often it means to endure pressures or to endure under pressure.

---

[15] Jennings, *Lexicon to the Syriac New Testament*, p. 146.

Chapter 6 ∴ Forbearing One Another in Love

I believe there are four aspects to forbearing: 1) holding under, 2) holding up, 3) holding back and 4) holding on.

HOLDING UNDER

This aspect of forbearing is regarding our relationship with people, especially other believers. We help to support and sustain one another, like a ship is undergirded with ropes or buoyed up. I picture having an arm around the shoulder of a friend in time of need. Some synonyms for this kind of forbearing might be comforting, supporting, strengthening and cheering up.

> *2 Thessalonians 1:3-4 APNT*
> *3 We are indebted to give thanks to God always for you, my brothers, as is right, because your faith grows abundantly and the love of each one of you increases for his associate,*
> *4 so that we will also be boasting about you among the churches of God concerning your faith and concerning your endurance in all your persecution and your trials that you are enduring.*

An example of this was very vivid to me when my husband was sick last year. He needed a lot of support in being able to get back on his feet and able to do simple functions again. I was the "shoulder" he leaned on.

HOLDING UP

Now let's look at a few of the verses where the noun based on the verb *sevar* is used. The noun is *mesaibranutha* and is translated both patience and forbearance. It's amazing how much forbearance is tied with longsuffering.

> *Romans 5:3 APNT*
> *And not only so, but we also boast in our adversities, because we know that adversity perfects patience [mesaibranutha] in us,*

Chapter 6 ∴ Forbearing One Another in Love

Here it is translated "patience" but it could also be "endurance." Adversity perfects endurance in us, and endurance, experience, and experience, hope. Hope is definitely tied in together with this word and when an Aramaic speaking person hears the word *mesaibranutha* it has *sevar* in it in the actual speaking of that word, so it immediately leads one's thoughts to the Hope of Christ's return. Without the Hope it would be impossible to have this kind of patience on an extended basis.

> *Romans 8:25 APNT*
> *But if we hope [sevar] for something that is not seen, we continue with endurance [mesaibranutha].*

We wait with endurance and as we wait, we intertwine our hearts together with God's heart. If our hearts are completely united with God's, then we will be able to endure through every situation because we know that the Hope of Christ's return is certain. We will also be able to hold up others, especially in times of grief or sorrow. It is a crucial element of action in our walking worthy of our calling.

1 Timothy is written to a young minister and it talks about pursuing this concept.

> *1 Timothy 6:11 APNT*
> *But you, oh man of God, flee from these [things] and pursue after justification and after uprightness and after faith and after love and after patience and after meekness.*

Forbearance is one of the things that we are to pursue along with the other things listed there, and it is available for us to have it in our lives. Some people might say, "Well, I'm just not a patient person." But forbearance is also a fruit of the spirit (Galatians 5:22), which is one of the characteristics of Christ in us. It is a matter of realizing that we can truly have this kind of endurance by the Spirit.

Chapter 6 ∴ Forbearing One Another in Love

HOLDING BACK

When combined with longsuffering (pouring out the breath and giving it time), endurance has the idea of time as well. It is almost a continuation where you pour out the breath and <u>then</u> you just hold on through thick and thin.

Forbearance is not only a fruit of the Spirit but it is also a quality that God says he has. He says that he is a God of patience.

> *Romans 15:5 APNT*
> *Now the God of patience [mesaibranutha] and of comfort grant you to think in harmony with each other, in Jesus Christ,*

What forbearance is not is stoicism, leniency, hastiness or ill temper. It is instead how God has dealt with our former sins. He held back what we justly deserved. Now we should be imitators of him.

> *Romans 3:25-26 ESV*
> *25 whom God put forward as a propitiation by his blood, to be received by faith. This was to show God's righteousness, because in his divine forbearance he had passed over former sins.*
> *26 It was to show his righteousness at the present time, so that he might be just and the justifier of the one who has faith in Jesus.*

HOLDING ON

The scriptures tell us what we should think in our minds so we can hold on in any kind of situation.

> *Romans 15:4 APNT*
> *For everything that was previously written is for our instruction. It was written so that by the patience and by the comfort of the scriptures we would have hope.*

Chapter 6 ∴ Forbearing One Another in Love

God's promises are always true and they always come to pass, but sometimes there is some holding on that needs to be done before we actually receive the promise. We talked about that in light of Abraham with longsuffering. We have the Hope of Christ's return, but we also live in the hope of receiving answers on a daily basis in order to deal with the trials that come our way. Hope is an expectation that victory is coming. This is an important element of forbearance and is the opposite of being resigned to struggle.

> *Hebrews 12:1 APNT*
> *Because of this also, we, who have all these witnesses that surround us like a cloud, should unfasten all our burdens from us, even the sin that is always prepared for us, and we should run with patience this race that is set for us.*

In order to "run the race" we need forbearance. You can see this in terms of running a race, as running a marathon. It takes a tremendous amount of preparation and training, and in the process of actually going through it, it takes endurance to make it all the way through without giving up. This is a quality that we need to encourage one another about. Sometimes people give up in the middle before receiving the promises. In ministering situations this is a quality that is needed.

> *2 Corinthians 6:4 APNT*
> *But in everything we should show ourselves that we are ministers of God with much endurance, in trials, in necessities, in difficulties,*

"Holding on" is to bear on our shoulders with faith things we cannot control and our response is to be in love, seeking God's grace in the situation.

> *James 1:3-4 APNT*
> *3 for you know that the experience of faith causes you to obtain patience.*

Chapter 6 ∴ Forbearing One Another in Love

4 Now patience should have a full work that you may be mature and complete and not lacking in anything.

We need to believe in the midst of numerous trials. Forbearance or endurance should have a "full work." Endurance is a quality in our lives that demonstrates maturity.

James 1:12 APNT
Blessed [is] the man who endures trials, so that when he is examined, he may receive the crown of life that God promised to those who love him.

The crown of life certainly has to do with the rewards we will receive throughout eternity. I believe it is also talking about the reward in life now when we endure trials, because when we endure, we prove (experience) the comfort, encouragement and strengthening that God provides in order to help us to continue holding on. God promises this to those who love him.

Forbearing one another in love is the first thing we need to do in order to walk worthy of our calling. We need to be holding and helping to support one another. We need to be holding each other up with love, while keeping the long view of the Hope in mind.

1 Corinthians 13:7 APNT
[Love] endures [sevar in Paiel] everything, believes everything, hopes [sevar] all, bears all.

We need to be holding back, as God does with us and we need to be holding on, controlling our thinking and lining it up with God's promises, while continually wrapping our hearts around God's heart. We can help to bear one another's load and continue to hope and have an expectation that answers are coming. There is great reward if we pursue this quality of forbearance.

Chapter 7 ❖ Endeavoring to Keep Unity

The second participle that we are going to consider is "endeavoring." And we are posing the questions, what does unity mean and how do we keep it?

> *Ephesians 4:3 KJV*
> *Endeavouring to keep the unity of the Spirit in the bond of peace.*

Endeavoring is the Greek word, *spoudazo*. It means to "make haste, especially as manifested in diligence, earnestness; to do the utmost."[16] I love the translation of this verse from the Complete Jewish Bible.

> *Ephesians 4:3 CJB*
> *and making every effort to preserve the unity the Spirit gives through the binding power of shalom.*

We need to make every effort to keep or preserve the unity of the Spirit. Right away we see that unity is not something we can manufacture of ourselves. It comes by way of the Spirit of God who made us one. In verses 4-6, there are seven ways we share in oneness.

> *Ephesians 4:4-6 APNT*
> *4 so that you will be in one body and by one Spirit, even as you are called in one hope of your calling.*
> *5 For [there] is one Lord and one faith and one baptism*
> *6 and one God, the Father of all and above all and by all and in us all.*

This oneness is like a unit of measure and since all believers have this same measure, we have a common ground and touchpoint with every other believer. The Aramaic translation adds some insight to help us understand unity.

---

[16] Bullinger, *A Critical Lexicon and Concordance*, p. 224.

Chapter 7 ∴ Endeavoring to Keep Unity

Ephesians 4:3 APNT
and be diligent to keep the alliance of the Spirit with the girdle of
peace,

We can learn what the concept means by identifying the root verb and its action. The abstract concept is linked with this action and can be understood more thoroughly by looking at the root action. Unity comes from a verb root in Aramaic that means simply "to turn towards a place or person with affection." An intensive form of the verb means, "to unite or reconcile."[17] An example of this verb usage is in Matthew 5.

Matthew 5:25 KJV
Agree with thine adversary quickly, whiles thou art in the way with
him; lest at any time the adversary deliver thee to the judge and the
judge deliver thee to the officer, and thou be cast into prison.

The Aramaic root verb, *aoa*, is the word "agree." Obviously, if the man in this verse agreed already, it would not call his opponent an adversary and they would not be on the way to the court. Agree here means "to settle or reconcile, to make an alliance." The way that is done can be seen in this verse. Stop on the road, sit down, turn towards one another, talk things out and cause an alliance to be made. This alliance is "of the Spirit."

When a believer turns to another believer with interest and affection, what should happen is an instant recognition that the other has THE SAME HOLY SPIRIT in them!

Ephesians 2:18 KJV
For through him we both have access by one Spirit unto the Father.

That same Spirit is the touchpoint that stirs our interest and desire to form some kind of bond. It is the "bond of peace." Ephesians 2:13-14

---

[17] J. Payne Smith, *A Compendious Syriac Dictionary,* p. 4.

tell us how we have peace "in Jesus Christ." He is our peace because he broke down the separations between Jew and Gentile, bond and free, male and female (see also Galatians 3:28). Ephesians 2:17 says that "he came and he declared peace to you." There is peace because of the one Spirit! The Aramaic word for peace in Ephesians 2:15 is not the normal word for peace, but it means "peace treaty." Sound like the word for unity? I believe it has the same idea or picture. Jesus Christ formed a peace treaty between the Jews and Gentiles because he gave the same gift of the Spirit to each one.

Peace in the New Testament is also used in the context of the body of Christ and living the mystery. The gospel or glad tidings of peace are that each believer has the Spirit born in them, but also that they have a special place in a body. They are members in particular. It brings peace to know that your particular place is unique in the body of Christ. There is no competition or vying for position because the head, the Lord Jesus Christ, directs your unique function.

When we "turn to someone with interest or affection" and realize he is a believer, we recognize that he has the same gift of the Spirit and the same Lord we do. That gives us a touchpoint that helps us to hurdle any of the other differences. Then we rejoice because we can also recognize the "Christ in" the other person and how we each have a special place and function in the body of Christ. We can then promote that unity with love, tying relationships together and developing in maturity, promoting a peace treaty. This is keeping the unity of the Spirit in the bond of peace.

To summarize the points made thus far: "endeavoring" is the action and "to keep" is something we already have but need to preserve. The cause of our unity is based on the fact that each believer has the same gift of the Spirit that is the measure of Christ (Ephesians 4:7) and each believer is a member in particular in the body of Christ (1 Corinthians 12:27).

Chapter 7 ∴ Endeavoring to Keep Unity

The word for bond in Ephesians 4:3 gives more insight about how we can promote unity. It can be translated girdle or band. A girdle holds something together. The only other place in the New Testament where this word girdle is used is in Colossians 3:14 (APNT): "And with all these [things], [put on] love, which is the girdle of maturity." Maturity characterizes a person who puts on the girdle of love. Love enables us to walk and to carry on our own business. Love binds people together. Love is the mark of a mature Christian.

There are five uses of the Aramaic noun *auyutha* that are built from the root verb *aoa*. They reveal some principles involved in walking in harmony with God and his family. The first use is translated "alliance."

> *2 Corinthians 6:16 APNT*
> *And what alliance [auyutha] has the temple of God with demons? But you are the temple of the living God, as it is said: I will live with them and I will walk with them and I will be their God and they will be my people.*

The temple of the living God is the body of Christ. There is no harmony possible between the body of Christ and people who worship other gods. Basically, idolatry is putting anything or anyone ahead of God. If a person is not putting God first, he will not be able to "pull together" in harmony with someone who is. One of the biggest idols is "self."

The second use shows that we can always find something to rejoice about together in the body of Christ.

> *2 Corinthians 13:11 APNT*
> *From now on, my brothers, rejoice and be mature and be comforted and there will be agreement [auyutha] and harmony [peace treaty] among you and the God of love and of peace will be with you.*

But what about when there is a disagreement, whether doctrinally or with a certain practice? The answer is to "love your neighbor as yourself." T.D. Jakes has a very famous quote about viewing others as a "work in progress." He said, "We have a tendency to want the other person to be a finished product while we give ourselves the grace to evolve."[18]

The third use is the one we are discussing in Ephesians 4:3. Remember that it is our job to be diligent to preserve the harmony given to us by the Spirit.

The fourth use of *auyutha* is in Philippians 3:16, but let's read the whole context.

> *Philippians 3:12-16 APNT*
> *12 I have not yet received [the victory], nor yet been made perfect, but I am running, so that I will attain what Jesus Christ attained [for] me.*
> *13 My brothers, I do not consider myself to have attained. But one [thing] I know, that I am forgetting what is behind me and I am reaching out before me.*
> *14 And I am running toward the goal, so that I would receive the victory of the high calling of God in Jesus Christ.*
> *15 Therefore, those who are mature should think these [things] and if you think anything otherwise, God will also reveal this to you.*
> *16 Nevertheless, to reach this, we should follow in one path and with one agreement [auyutha].*

None of us have attained the goal of becoming exactly like Christ. But we can forget those things that are behind and pursue the prize of the high calling.

The whole book of Philippians has a lot to share about being of one accord. Here are two sections.

---

[18] www.azquotes.com/author/7311-T_D_Jakes/tag/grace

Chapter 7 ∴ Endeavoring to Keep Unity

Philippians 1:27 APNT
Conduct yourselves as is becoming to the gospel of Christ, so that if I
come, I may see you and if I am distant, I may hear about you, that you
are standing in one spirit and in one soul and [that] you are conquering
together in the faith of the gospel.

Philippians 2:1-4 APNT
1 Therefore, if you have encouragement in Christ or if [you have]
consolation in love or if [you have] fellowship of the Spirit or if [you
have] loving-kindness and mercies,
2 complete my joy, so that you will have one mind and one love and one
soul and one purpose.
3 And do not do anything with controversy or with empty boasting, but
with humbleness of mind. Everyone should count his associate as better
than himself.
4 And a man should not be concerned for himself [only], but each one
[should] also [be concerned] for his associate.

Doesn't verse 3 sound like meekness and longsuffering?

The last use of *auyutha* is in 1 Peter and shows more about how to be of
one mind.

1 Peter 3:8-11 APNT
8 Now the conclusion [is] that all of you should be in agreement
[auyutha] and you should suffer with those who suffer and be
compassionate to one another and you should be merciful and humble.
9 And you should not repay anyone evil for evil, nor abuse for abuse,
but in contrast to these [things], bless, for you were called to this, so
that you may inherit a blessing.
10 Therefore, he who desires life and loves to see good days should keep
his tongue from evil and his lips should speak no deceit.
11 He should turn away from evil and do good and should seek peace
and pursue it,

Similar exhortations are given in Ephesians regarding the words that we speak: speak the truth in love (4:15), speak every man truth with his neighbor (4:25) and speak that which ministers grace to the hearers (4.29).

I believe that Colossians has a great summary of what we have been talking about with keeping the unity of the Spirit in the bond of peace and love.

> *Colossians 3:12-17 APNT*
> *12 Therefore, as the chosen [ones] of God, holy and beloved, put on mercies and loving-kindness and gentleness and humbleness of mind and quietness and long-suffering.*
> *13 And be forbearing to one another and forgiving to one another. And if someone has a complaint against his associate, as Christ forgave you, so also you forgive.*
> *14 And with all these [things], [put on] love, which is the girdle of maturity.*
> *15 And the peace of Christ will govern your hearts, for to him you were called in one body. And be thankful to Christ,*
> *16 that his word may live in you richly with all wisdom. And teach and instruct yourselves in psalms and in hymns and in songs of the Spirit and sing with grace in your hearts to God.*
> *17 And everything that you do in word and in work, do in the name of our Lord Jesus Christ and give thanks by way of him to God the Father.*

When peace governs our hearts, we realize that every single believer is called by God to be an important member of the body of Christ. We each have a special place and no one is left out. We can be thankful for this unity and continue to teach and encourage each other how to walk in it.

Chapter 8 ❖ Walking in Love

In previous chapters we have talked about how love is a crucial aspect of our walk. Let's look a little deeper so we can grasp what God's love is. We are to imitate God as his loved sons and daughters.

> *Ephesians 5:1-2 APNT*
> *1 Therefore, imitate God as beloved sons.*
> *2 And walk in love, as Christ also loved us and delivered himself up for us, an offering and a sacrifice to God for a sweet smell.*

In this verse, it is clear that our example is Christ who gave up his life for us and on our behalf. Love, as openly seen in Christ, is given as the motive and the pattern of the love that should mark our walk.

The Aramaic word for love is *khuba*. It is derived from the root verb *khav* meaning "to be kindled, set on fire, burn fiercely, thus to love vehemently, embrace, cherish."[19] The action of kindling a fire has to do with breathing on it. Here is the word picture in the old Hebrew letters, reading right to left, kheth and beth.

house – fence

The following are the definitions of these letters from the Analytical Hebrew Lexicon:

> The first character (reading right to left) is a picture of a wall. The second one is a picture of a tent or house. The walls of the house enclose the home as refuge for the family. A refuge functions as a place of hiding from any undesirable person or

---

[19] J. Payne Smith, *A Compendious Syriac Dictionary*, p. 122.

situation. Other meanings for this parent root include: bosom, a place where one is hidden in the arms and cherished.[20]

The simple word picture for love is **the fence of the family**. Love is a place of shelter. One time when I was teaching this, we spontaneously displayed it by surrounding someone who had a need and encircled her and then ministered to her as a group. It was very powerful!

A wall or fence guards someone, so others cannot hurt the family. Children are hidden in our arms and cherished. They want to be close to their parents because then they feel safe.

The related Hebrew word is *khabab* meaning to love fervently, hold close to the bosom, to cherish. *Khabab* is used only one time in the Old Testament in Deuteronomy 33:3 where Moses blessed the children of Israel before his death. He said, "Yea, he [the LORD] loved [*khabab*] the people; all his saints are in thy hand: and they sat down at thy feet; every one shall receive of thy words." The picture is of God holding the holy ones (his people) close to his bosom and cherishing them. He took care of them from the time they left Egypt for more than 40 years and guided them by the pillar of fire at night and the cloud by day.

Although this word is used only once in the Old Testament, the imagery of God loving or cherishing his people by holding or carrying them in his bosom is found elsewhere in both the Old and New Testaments.

> *Isaiah 40:11 ESV*
> *He will tend his flock like a shepherd; he will gather the lambs in his arms; he will carry them in his bosom, and gently lead those that are with young.*

The shepherd wore a large outer mantle that usually had a fold sewn in it. When a lamb was sick or needed tending, the shepherd would lift the

---

[20] Benner, *Ancient Hebrew Lexicon of the Bible*, p. 117.

lamb up into the fold or "pocket" of his mantle where he could rub oil on a wound or just allow the lamb to rest. The is the idea of "carry them in his bosom."

We, his beloved saints, are also in the bosom of God with Christ, in his love and care.

> *Colossians 3:3b APNT*
> *...your life is hidden with Christ in God.*

Another related Hebrew word to *khav* which is used many times in the Old Testament is *ahav*. It means to provide for the family, protect or guard. In this way, love is giving and "to give" is also a related word. I chose one verse using *ahav* to illustrate it for you.

> *Zephaniah 3:17 ESV*
> *The LORD your God is in your midst, a mighty one who will save; he will rejoice over you with gladness; he will quiet you by his love; he will exult over you with loud singing.*

So far we have learned that love is a wall around the family where they can be nurtured and cherished. Love holds someone close to the bosom and then provides the protection and care needed. Love quiets us.

Since we are talking about our walk, how do we walk in love? How do we look for what is the need? What's the provision that needs to happen in the house? There is an interesting verse in Deuteronomy about how God kept Israel as the apple of his eye. And since we are to be imitators of God as dear children, this is one way we can love.

> *Deuteronomy 32:9-10 ESV*
> *9 But the LORD's portion is his people, Jacob his allotted heritage.*

Chapter 8 ∴ Walking in Love

10 "He found him in a desert land, and in the howling waste of the wilderness; he encircled him, he cared for him, he kept him as the apple of his eye."

The phrase about "the apple of his eye" literally means the little man in the eye, and the word apple is a pupil. When you look directly in someone's eye, you actually see a reflection of yourself or "a little man." God is looking directly into our eyes so that our lives will be right there in his vision and he keeps us close by. The eyelids are designed to protect the retina and pupil and to prevent anything from falling in the eye to disturb it. And the eyelashes also have short hairs to break off the rays of the light which sometimes would be too strong for the pupil.

The Lord kept and guarded Israel while they were passing through the wilderness so that no one was hurt. He provided manna for them to eat each day and their clothes did not even wear out. This is one way we can love – by keeping each other in our sight and endeavoring to guard and protect one another. If God did this for Israel, will he not do even more for us because we are his children?

Ephesians 2:4-6 APNT
4 But God, who is rich in his mercies, because of his great love [khuba] with which he loved [khav] us,
5 while we were dead in our sins, gave us life with Christ and, by his grace, redeemed us
6 and raised us up with him and seated us with him in heaven in Jesus Christ.

The great love of God is poured out into our hearts by way of the Spirit. The love of God has flooded us within and we have God's nature born within us.

Romans 5:5-10 APNT
5 And hope does not put [us] to shame, because the love of God is poured out in our hearts by the Holy Spirit that was given to us.
6 Now if Christ at this time, because of our weakness, died for the ungodly,
7 (for seldom does anyone die for the ungodly, although for good [ones] perhaps some would dare to die)
8 here God has manifested his love that is toward us, because if when we were sinners, Christ died for us,
9 then how much more will we be justified now by his blood and be rescued from wrath by him?
10 For if when we were enemies God was reconciled with us by the death of his Son, then how much more will we by his reconciliation live by his life?

God loved us even when we were enemies and sinners! That kind of love is already in our hearts and we can love the unlovable also.

Like God cherishing us in his bosom, so Paul compared the love and care that he and Silas and Timothy showed the Thessalonians to that of a nursing mother loving her children. It was the fruit of the Spirit love and people observed their tender care.

1 Thessalonians 2:7-8 APNT
7 But we were meek among you, and as a nurse who loves [khav] her children,
8 so also we were loving [khav] and were desiring to give to you not only the gospel of God, but also ourselves, because you were beloved [khabiva].

There is so much more that could be said about love and we will continue to come back to this topic throughout the rest of the book because love should be a thread through every aspect of our lives. We would be remiss if we did not include verses from 1 Corinthians 13 that show the qualities we should seek to have because we love. Love never fails — it never falls to the ground and does nothing.

> *1 Corinthians 13:4-8a APNT*
> *4 Love is long-suffering and kind. Love does not envy. Love is not ruffled and is not puffed up*
> *5 and does not do that which is shameful and does not seek its own and is not enraged and does not think what is evil,*
> *6 does not rejoice in wickedness, but rejoices with truthfulness.*
> *7 [Love] endures everything, believes everything, hopes all, bears all.*
> *8 Love never fails.*

At one time a wonderful believer made this picture for me that summarizes some of the things we have been talking about concerning love. Please enjoy it as well.

Chapter 9 ❖ Walk According to the Spirit

We have mentioned a number of times how our walk is together with all the other believers in the world. In this chapter we are going to look at how we can live that life according to the Spirit.

> *2 Corinthians 1:21-22 APNT*
> *21 Now God establishes us with you in Christ, who anointed us*
> *22 and has sealed us and has placed the down payment of his Spirit in our hearts.*

Often, we think about how it is "Christ in me" and do not realize that the pronoun "you" can be plural. It is not evident in English whether the pronoun "you" is plural or singular. In the verse above, God establishes "us," and "you" is plural. He has placed the down payment of his Spirit in "our" hearts.

> *Colossians 1:26-27 APNT*
> *26 the mystery that was hidden from ages and from generations, but now is revealed to his holy [ones].*
> *27 To them, God wanted to make known what is the wealth of the glory of this mystery among the Gentiles, which is the Messiah who is in you, the hope of our glory,*

The wealth of the glory of the mystery of the church of the body is that we all together have Christ the Messiah in US. The word Christ means "anointed one" and the anointing we have is the fullness of the Spirit that was on Jesus Christ. We each have this fullness, so we are joined together with this special touchpoint of commonality. When we start thinking about the walk by the Spirit as something we do together, it changes our perspective. We are walking together, not as individuals only. Certainly, we each need to apply our hearts to walking, but for example, when I need to have some power manifested in my life, I can rely on a brother or sister to walk by the Spirit with me and help me.

Chapter 9 ∴ Walk According to the Spirit

Ephesians 1:11-14 APNT
11 And we were chosen in him, even as he marked us out beforehand and he desired, he who performs everything according to the purpose of his will,
12 that we, those who first trusted in Christ, should be for the esteem of his magnificence.
13 In him also, you heard the word of truthfulness, which is the gospel of your life, and in him, you believed and you were sealed with the Holy Spirit that was promised,
14 which is the guarantee of our inheritance to the redemption of those who have life and to the glory of his honor.

This section in Ephesians is reiterating that WE were sealed with the Spirit that was promised. And this is a guarantee that WE will all receive the inheritance together. As we go through some of the ways we walk by the Spirit this will become clearer.

Sometimes in the New Testament it says to walk in something and sometimes it says to walk by something and it also can be according to something. We looked at a few of them already, walking in the light and walking in love. In Greek there are a number of prepositions that are very specific. In the following verse, the preposition is *kata*, which means according to, or down from.

Romans 8:1 KJV
There is therefore now no condemnation to them which are in Christ Jesus, who walk not after the flesh, but after the Spirit.

Normally, in the King James Version, the walk is described as "in" the Spirit. But in most modern translations, it says walk "by" the Spirit.

Galatians 5:16 KJV
This I say then, Walk in the Spirit, and ye shall not fulfil the lust of the flesh.

Chapter 9 ⋮⋮ Walk According to the Spirit

Galatians 5:16 NET
But I say, live by the Spirit and you will not carry out the desires of the flesh.

In Aramaic, there is only one preposition and it can mean in, by, with, according to, towards. It is a really broad preposition. What I started looking at was the way we normally say we walk by the Spirit. If we change it up in our minds and instead of putting the preposition "by," put "in" or put "according to," we get a whole different idea. Let's talk about walking in love meaning we dwell IN love. God is love and we dwell in his presence. But now make it walking BY love. Remember when we were discussing *stoicheo* in chapter 2 where we walk BY the same rule.

Philippians 3:16 KJV
Nevertheless, whereto we have already attained, let us walk by the same rule, let us mind the same thing.

What is the rule? One of the things is love. We walk so love becomes a standard by which we live.

We can also say ACCORDING TO love and then the emphasis is about how I practically live out the love. It's not only that God has loved me in Christ, but how do I live that love with my fellow members of the family?

I prepared a chart for further study and you can apply what I am talking about to each one of these categories. We can do that with every single one of these and it will give us a completely different idea. Another brief example is wisdom. We can walk IN wisdom because Christ is made unto us wisdom. We have it inside and we need to meditate on that. But then we can also live BY wisdom where it becomes our rule and our practice, what we base our life on. Then we can walk ACCORDING TO wisdom also and that becomes the practical application.

Positive	Negative
Light (1 John 1:7)	Darkness (John 8:12; John 11:10)
Truth (2 John 1:4; 3 John 1:3-4)	Craftiness (2 Corinthians 4:2)
Love (Ephesians 5:2)	Strife (1 Corinthians 3:3)
Wisdom (Colossians 4:5)	Vanity of Own Mind (Ephesians 4:17)
Newness of Life (Romans 6:4)	Own Ways (Acts 14:16)
Spirit (Galatians 5:16)	Flesh (2 Corinthians 10:2; Romans 8:1-4)
Believing Faith (Galatians 3:11)	Sight (2 Corinthians 5:7)
God's Commandments (2 John 1:6)	Course of this World – Evil (Ephesians 2:2; 2 Thessalonians 3:6, 11)

Now that we know this about the prepositions, let us apply it to walking by the Spirit.

> *Galatians 5:16-18, 25 APNT*
> *16 But I say, "Walk by the Spirit and never serve the desire of the flesh."*
> *17 For the flesh desires what is opposed to the Spirit and the Spirit desires what is opposed to the flesh, and the two of them are opposites to each other, so that you are not doing what you want.*
> *18 Now if you are led by the Spirit, you are not under the law.*
> *25 Therefore, we should live by the Spirit and we should follow the Spirit.*

Verses 16 and 18 are about being led BY the Spirit. But then verse 25 is about dwelling IN the Spirit and following the Spirit.

> *Romans 8:11-14 APNT*
> *11 And if the Spirit of that one who raised our Lord Jesus Christ from the dead lives in you, that one who raised Jesus Christ from the dead*

will also make alive your dead bodies because of his Spirit that lives in you.
12 Now, my brothers, we are not debtors to the flesh that we should walk in the flesh.
13 For if you live by the flesh, you are going to die. And if spiritually you put to death the habits of the body, you will have life.
14 For those who are led by the Spirit of God are the sons of God.

This section in Romans 8 is referring to our walk according to the Spirit, where it becomes a lifestyle practically. We already are the sons of God, but our sonship is manifested to ourselves and others as we change the way we walk from our five senses (flesh) to the Spirit of God.

The use of "flesh" in Romans 8 and other places is a figure of speech, metonymy, where flesh represents the senses, our natural life.

A very important principle of walking and learning to live according to the Spirit is that there are five spiritual senses in Christ in the inner man, just as there are five physical senses. If I walk according to the physical senses, I am either going to see, hear, taste, touch or smell something. My spiritual senses are the same. I have spiritual ears. I have spiritual eyes. I have spiritual touch. When God wants to communicate to me and I want to talk to him, he is doing it by way of those spiritual senses. Just think for a moment now about our physical senses. When I look at you and see you or even just hear you, it doesn't take very long before my brain registers a recognition of who you are. That is the same way that the spiritual senses work. We don't have to analyze whether we hear a voice or we see a vision or whatever. When the spiritual senses are working then there is a recognition of something and it is not that important how we received it.

One time when I was learning about how to receive revelation like that, we were having a fellowship and there was a horrible smell in the room. I looked at my husband and whispered to him to ask if he smelled it. He

Chapter 9 ∵ Walk According to the Spirit

said "No" and I was so perplexed because it was a very bad smell. Then God showed me that there was a man in the room who had a devil spirit and that spirit was not happy that he was in the fellowship. As soon as I recognized what was happening, the smell went away. That spiritual sense of smell has happened on other occasions as well.

I said it is not that important how we receive from our spiritual senses, but when we are first learning to walk by the Spirit, it is a key thing to understand. David Guzik has a commentary of the whole Bible and he used an illustration of walking by the Spirit. "It's as if we are a computer, and we have two hard drives in us. One is programmed according to the Spirit, and the other is programmed according to the flesh. In any given situation, it's up to us to decide which 'drive' we will access. The resources of the Spirit are there. The resources of the flesh are there - but which will you access? Some want to take the 'drive' of their flesh and make it as efficient as possible. God never meant your system to run that way. He wants you to run off the 'drive' of the Spirit of God."[21]

All the resources of the Spirit are on that hard drive and all we have to do is plug into it. We are not designed to rely on the resources of the flesh. The most efficient way for our "computer" to work is to access and rely on the Spirit of God. God designed our physical bodies and soul to actually be subservient to him, as that hard drive of the flesh gets put underneath the Spirit of God hard drive. And when we choose the Spirit of God it starts running the other drive and has the priority.

Let's end this chapter by looking at the record in Acts 10 of Simon Peter witnessing to the first Gentile believers in the household of Cornelius and we will see these spiritual senses in action.

---

[21] Guzik, *Enduring Word* Commentary, E-Sword, Galatians 5:1-26.

Chapter 9 ∴ Walk According to the Spirit

Acts 10:9-16 APNT

9 And on the next day, while they were traveling on the journey and approaching the city, Simon went up to the roof to pray at the sixth hour.

10 And he was hungry and wanted to eat. And while they were preparing for him, astonishment came on him

11 and he saw heaven opened and a certain garment being held by four corners. And it was like a large linen cloth and it was coming down from heaven to the earth.

12 And in it there were many four-footed animals and creeping things of the earth and birds of heaven.

13 And a voice came to him that said, "Simon, rise up, kill and eat."

14 And Simon said, "Let it not be so, my Lord, because I have never eaten anything that is corrupt and unclean."

15 And again a second time, a voice came to him, "That which God has cleansed, do not regard as corrupt."

16 And this happened three times and the garment was lifted up to heaven.

First God gave Peter a vision of a large linen cloth with unclean animals in it and instructed Peter to eat of them. He saw this vision with his spiritual eyes.

Acts 10:17-20 APNT

17 And while Simon wondered in himself what was the vision that he had seen, those men who had been sent by Cornelius arrived. And they asked for the house in which Simon lodged and they came and stood at the gate of the courtyard.

18 And they called there and asked, "Is Simon, who is called Peter, lodged here?"

19 And while Simon thought on the vision, the Spirit said to him, "Behold, three men seek you.

20 Rise up, get down, and go with them, not letting your mind doubt, because I have sent them."

Chapter 9 ∴ Walk According to the Spirit

Then when the men sent from Cornelius arrived at Peter's house, Peter heard a spiritual voice that told him to go with the men. This is one way that sometimes revelation is described: "the Spirit said to him."

> *Acts 10:28 APNT*
> *And he said to them, "You know that it is not lawful for a Judean man to associate with an alien man who is not [of] his race, yet God showed me that I should not say about anyone that he is unclean or corrupt.*

After Peter came to Cornelius' house, he said that God had shown him a partial explanation of the vision. God had revealed to him that he should not get upset about being at a Gentile house. Then as Peter began to speak, he said that he perceived something. This was the recognition of what God had been wanting to tell him.

> *Acts 10:34-36 APNT*
> *34 And Simon opened his mouth and said, "In truth, I perceive that God is not a respecter of persons,*
> *35 but among all the nations, he who fears him and works uprightness is acceptable to him.*
> *36 For [this is] the word that he sent to the sons of Israel and declared to them: Peace and harmony by way of Jesus Christ, who is the Lord of all.*

You can finish reading the record because on this Gentile household the gift of the Spirit was poured out as it had been on the day of Pentecost and they spoke in tongues and were magnifying God. After Peter came back to Joppa, he told the believers what had happened and they praised God.

> *Acts 11:15-18 APNT*
> *15 And as I began to speak there, the Holy Spirit overshadowed them, as [it had] previously on us.*

Chapter 9 ∴ Walk According to the Spirit

16 And I remembered the word of our Lord, who said, 'John baptized with water, but you will be baptized with the Holy Spirit.'
17 Therefore, if God equally gave the gift to the Gentiles that believed in our Lord Jesus Christ, as also to us, who was I that I should be able to hinder God?"
18 And after they had heard these words, they were quiet and praised God and were saying, "Doubtless, God has also given repentance to life to the Gentiles."

What we have seen in this chapter is that we walk together by the Spirit in a family. We can use the prepositions in, by and according to for help in understanding how to walk by the Spirit. We walk in this way by God energizing our spiritual senses.

Chapter 10 ❖ Evidence of the Spirit: A Way of Life

When we are walking by the Spirit, then there will be evidence of that in our lives. In this chapter we will explore the nine manifestations that are listed in 1 Corinthians 12. We are going to study these passages primarily from the Aramaic translation.

> *1 Corinthians 12:1-3 APNT*
> *1 Now about spiritual [things], my brothers, I want you to know*
> *2 that you were heathens and were led to idols that have no distinct voice.*
> *3 Because of this, I make known to you that there is no one who speaks by the Spirit of God and says that Jesus is cursed. And neither is anyone able to say that Jesus is Lord, except by the Holy Spirit.*

Chapters 12-14 in 1 Corinthians are all about spiritual matters or things. When we were not born again, we were led to idols, but now we can speak and preach that Jesus is Lord. In the next verses we are going to learn about distributions.

> *1 Corinthians 12:4-6 APNT*
> *4 And there are distributions of gifts, but the Spirit is one.*
> *5 And there are distributions of services, but the LORD is one.*
> *6 And there are distributions of powers, but God is the one who works all in everyone.*

The word translated "distributions" means a dividing of something. I think distribution is a good translation because God is the one who distributes the active working of the Spirit in each believer in the body of Christ. These three verses are basically saying the same thing. No matter if we are talking about gifts or ways of serving or power, it is the Spirit of the Lord God who distributes them. And God is the one who energizes all the distributions.

Chapter 10 ∵ Evidence of the Spirit: A Way of Life

1 Corinthians 12:7 APNT
Now the manifestation of the Spirit is given to each one as it is
profitable for him.

Now the context shifts to begin to explain what the manifestation of the Spirit is. A manifestation is something evident or shown – a proof. An example would be that there is a pot boiling on the stove and we smell a delicious aroma coming from the kitchen. If we go to the kitchen and lift the lid of the pot, then the spaghetti sauce will be "evident." The manifestation of the Spirit "lifts the lid of the pot," so to speak. We cannot see the Spirit, but when we see the manifestation of it, then we know it came by way of that Spirit.

The manifestations of the Spirit are given to "each one" meaning that every believer can have all of these evidenced in his or her life. The last part of the verse is translated in the Aramaic "as it is profitable for him." Profitable is actually a present participle and shows that there is a figure of speech here of an ellipsis. We need to fill in something that "profiting" modifies. The figure would be like this: for a profiting _____. Some possibilities of what to fill in are situation, opportunity or time. The manifestations are given in a profiting situation where there would be a particular benefit. A simple way this might happen is when someone calls you up for advice but they are really sick and they end up receiving the manifestation of gifts of healing.

Now the passage continues to explain nine different "evidences" of what God can energize.

1 Corinthians 12:8 APNT
There is a word of wisdom that is given to him by the Spirit, now for
another, a word of knowledge by the same Spirit,

Notice that a word of wisdom is first and then a word of knowledge. It is crucial to understand what these are because they are opposite of how they are commonly used in English today. In order to understand the words, let's take a look at the word pictures with the ancient Hebrew pictographs.

The verb "to be wise," *khakem,* has three letters: kheth, caph and mem (read from right to left).

water – back of hand – fence

The fence is a door or can mean to separate. The back of the hand can mean source. And the mem is a picture of water, but also represents spiritual life. The word picture is **to separate out the source of the spiritual life**. Sources of life could be God, the devil, ourselves, someone else or even culture. In order to be wise, we need to know God's overall view of what is going on and his perspective on the source of the "facts." Is there truth or a lie? When we are talking about the manifestation of word of wisdom, this perspective is given by revelation for a specific situation.

The word for knowledge is *yada* and also has three letters: yoth, daleth and ayin.

eye – door – power

The yoth is a pictograph of a hand with the thumb raised and means hand or power, the work that the hand does. The daleth is a door and the ayin is the eye or what is experienced and seen. The word picture then is **the power of the door experienced** or how to go in the door. A word of knowledge is what to do in a specific situation that is going to be profiting.

Wisdom is first and then knowledge. When we ask the question "what do I do?" first, it is difficult to get the answer clearly. But if we ask for

Chapter 10 ∵ Evidence of the Spirit: A Way of Life

God's perspective and the source of what is going on first, then it is actually easy to know what to do.

Word of wisdom and word of knowledge are manifestations of the same kind (*allos* in Greek). But then follow five things which begin with *heteros* (another of a different kind) and they are all of the same kind. This group of five manifestations work together in various combinations in a profiting situation.

> *1 Corinthians 12:9-10a KJV*
> *9 To another [heteros] faith by the same Spirit; to another [allos] the gifts of healing by the same Spirit;*
> *10 To another [allos] the working of miracles; to another [allos] prophecy; to another [allos] discerning of spirits;*

I have developed some definitions of these five manifestations which are derived from multiple sources.

Faith – A surge of confidence that rises in a person in a particular situation and is an extraordinary certainty that God is about to act. This confidence is energized by God.

Gifts of healings – Presents of grace that cause healing physically, emotionally or spiritually.

Working(s) of miracles – (*dunamis* plural) – The effects of mighty works and powerful signs.

Prophecy – Pouring forth of words, actions or visions that bring life to the family. They are communicated from God to us to people.

Discerning of spirits – Becoming aware of spirits, especially evil spirits, and how to deal with them. We contend with and confront them in order to separate people from their influence and control. Also, there could be an awareness of the presence of the Spirit of God.

Chapter 10 ∴ Evidence of the Spirit: A Way of Life

God can energize any combination of those five manifestations. All are impossible to come to pass out of our own abilities or power. Please notice that prophecy and discerning of spirits are in this group and are included in impartation of some kind.

The list of nine manifestations in 1 Corinthians 12 concludes with two of the same kind.

> *1 Corinthians 12:10b KJV*
> *to another divers kinds of tongues; to another the interpretation of tongues:*

These evidences of the Spirit are energized by God as he purposes and desires. There is an active flow of God's power through us, active flowing energy.

> *1 Corinthians 12:11 APNT*
> *Now all these [things] the one Spirit works and distributes to everyone as he wills.*

This principle is reiterated in Hebrews.

> *Hebrews 2:3-4 APNT*
> *3 how will we escape, if we despise those [things] that are our life, those that began to be spoken by our Lord and were confirmed in us by those who heard,*
> *4 God being a witness about them with signs and with wonders and with various miracles and with distributions of the Holy Spirit that were given according to his will?*

Of course, God cannot energize something in us unless we are willing participants. There is a great verse in Philippians which explains how this works. When we desire to be in a profiting situation and to have God energize any combination of the manifestations, then God acts.

Philippians 2:13 APNT
For God energizes you to will (desire) as well as to perform what you desire.

You desire – God energizes.

With this background, let's look briefly at a record where there was a profiting opportunity. Four men brought a man who had "palsy" or was paralyzed to Jesus in Capernaum.

Mark 2:1-4 APNT
1 And Jesus again entered into Capernaum after [some] days. And when they heard that he was in the house,
2 many gathered, so that [the house] was not able to contain them, not even in front of the door. And he was speaking the word with them.
3 And they came to him and brought him a paralytic, bearing him between four [men].
4 And because they were not able to draw near to him because of the crowd, they climbed up to the roof and lifted the covering of the place where Jesus was and they lowered the bed on which the paralytic was laid.

The first thing we notice is that Jesus received a word of wisdom. He "saw" their (plural) faith.

Mark 2:5 APNT
And when Jesus saw their faith, he said to that paralytic, "My son, your sins are forgiven you."

Then Jesus immediately knew what to do (word of knowledge) and said prophetically, "Your sins are forgiven." Then the scribes and Pharisees who were there began reasoning in their hearts. Notice they did not speak anything out loud.

Chapter 10 ∴ Evidence of the Spirit: A Way of Life

> *Mark 2:6-9 APNT*
> *6 Now there were there some scribes and Pharisees, who were sitting and reasoning in their heart[s],*
> *7 "Why does this [man] speak blasphemy? Who is able to forgive sins, except one, God?"*
> *8 But Jesus knew in his spirit that they were reasoning these [things] in themselves and he said to them, "Why do you reason these [things] in your heart[s]?*
> *9 Which is easier to say to the paralytic, 'Your sins are forgiven you' or to say, 'Rise, take up your bed and walk?'*

Jesus received another word of wisdom ("he knew in his spirit") about what the scribes and Pharisees were thinking and immediately God gave him a word of knowledge of what to say to them. That is why I know that telling the man his sins were forgiven was prophecy. Neither is easier than the other to say, but Jesus said what the man needed to hear to receive his healing.

> *Mark 2:10-12 APNT*
> *10 But that you might know that it is lawful [for] the Son of Man to forgive sins on earth," he said to the paralytic,*
> *11 "I say to you, Rise, take up your bed, and go to your house."*
> *12 And he got up immediately and took his bed and went away in the sight of all, so that all of them were amazed and praised God, saying that they had never seen such.*

Jesus desired to heal the man and then God energized faith, working of miracles and gifts of healing all at the same time. If we examined many other records, especially of healings in the Bible, we would see how these manifestations all work together. When we are walking by the Spirit, any combination of these nine manifestations can be energized at any time.

Chapter 11 ❖ Wisdom and Knowledge

In the last chapter we saw that word of wisdom comes before word of knowledge in the way the manifestations of the Spirit work. And we need to desire and then God energizes any combination of those manifestations. Now I want to look a little bit deeper into what wisdom is and what knowledge is and how to get them.

WISDOM

Wisdom in the principal thing and getting wisdom is the primary thing to do. Remember that the word picture for wisdom is "to separate out the source of the spiritual life."

> *Proverbs 4:7 KJV*
> *Wisdom is the principal thing; therefore get wisdom: and with all thy getting get understanding.*

> *Proverbs 8:11 KJV*
> *For wisdom is better than rubies; and all the things that may be desired are not to be compared to it.*

The fear of the Lord is the beginning of both knowledge and wisdom. Fear means to have reverence and know that God is the source of all knowledge and all wisdom.

> *Proverbs 9:10 KJV*
> *The fear of the LORD is the beginning of wisdom: and the knowledge of the holy is understanding.*

Beginning is the word for starting point. Without God as our true starting point and foundation, we will not be able to receive his wisdom and knowledge. When we go to God and recognize our dependence on him as the only source, we get true wisdom and true knowledge.

Chapter 11 ∴ Wisdom and Knowledge

My children provided a good illustration of this concept. When my children were babies, I had to do a lot of work. I fed, clothed and cared for them. As they grew up to be teenagers, they wanted to make their own decisions. They said "I want to do this," and "I think this is important to have so I'm going to go get it, goodbye mom." As children they looked up to me and knew that they did not have the source of their own provision. As teenagers they wanted to provide for themselves. But teenagers as well as adults still need to go to their parents, especially their heavenly Father to provide wisdom. All of our attitudes towards God should not be those of a teenager but those of a child. We do not know everything and need God to direct our decisions. We always need to be dependent on God because he is the starting point and we must always go back to the starting point to have stability.

There are four key points about how to obtain wisdom that are illustrated in Proverbs.

> *Proverbs 2:1-5 NIV*
> *1 My son, if you accept my words and store up my commands within you,*
> *2 turning your ear to wisdom and applying your heart to understanding,*
> *3 indeed, if you call out for insight and cry aloud for understanding,*
> *4 and if you look for it as for silver and search for it as for hidden treasure,*
> *5 then you will understand the fear of the LORD and find the knowledge of God.*

In Hebrew poetry there are parallelisms. In each of these verses, there is a parallel. If you accept my words, then you store them up. Essentially, they are saying the same thing twice, except the second phrase is more intensified. By accepting God's Word, you have received them, but you can go further by storing them up like treasure. You can turn your ear to wisdom, but more intensely you can apply your heart to understanding. You can call out and you can more intensely cry aloud for understanding. You can not only look but diligently search.

The first key to receiving wisdom is having humility to accept the words of God. It is acknowledging God as the source, but also going further by accepting and keeping his words in our hearts. This requires a humble and meek heart. Humility is always wanting to learn and continuing to seek for the best answers. Remember, in chapter 5, we discussed that meekness is the first key to walking worthily.

> *James 3:13 KJV*
> *Who is a wise man and endued with knowledge among you? Let him show out of a good conversation his works with meekness of wisdom.*

The word for meekness in Aramaic means to lie down flat under something, as we saw previously. We are to lie down flat under God, looking up to him, ready to receive his wisdom, reproof, knowledge and love. Then we can store up his Word as a treasure in our hearts and keep seeking. In order to hear God, we must turn our ears toward him to listen.

The second key is applying our hearts to understanding. Turning and applying requires energy and effort. Understanding is the Hebrew word *bin*, meaning to separate or divide. We are able to divide and separate wisdom to mean something by having spiritual understanding. Our energy directed towards understanding produces an ability to discriminate. This paints a beautiful picture. Understanding is the fulcrum between wisdom and knowledge. It is important to recognize wisdom, but we need the balance of spiritual understanding in order to put it into practice effectively.

The third key to receiving wisdom is calling out to God and asking for him to supply it. God promises to supply if we just go to him and ask.

Chapter 11 ∴ Wisdom and Knowledge

James 1:5 ESV
If any of you lacks wisdom, let him ask God, who gives generously to all without reproach, and it will be given him.

Asking also requires humility and acknowledging God as the source of wisdom and understanding. It is simple to ask for something, but we must earnestly desire and trust that God will give us the answers we are seeking.

The final key is in Proverbs 2:4. If we look for wisdom as silver and search for it as hidden treasure, then we will have it. Colossians 2:3 says that the treasures of wisdom and knowledge are hid in God and Jesus Christ. It requires concerted effort to search for this treasure just as it takes effort to mine for silver. Understanding the orientalism of silver mining requires some searching in itself. In the East during that time explosives such as dynamite were not available. The tools used in mining were shovels and picks. People would first look for and then search the source of a river or a mountain where they thought there might be some silver or gold. Then they would follow the vein by continuing to dig and pick until eventually it became a mine. Job 28 shares more about how they mined for silver and describes an entire picture of searching for wisdom like hidden treasure. With this same attitude of heart, we should seek after the treasures in God's Word. God will show which direction to follow and where to look, and he will energize our efforts.

All the keys to acquiring wisdom (humility, understanding, asking and seeking) have a common thread: applied effort and dependence on God. God is the source of all life and in order to tap into that life we must know how to take the necessary steps and then act.

Job 28:20-23, 28 KJV
20 Whence then cometh wisdom? and where is the place of understanding?
21 Seeing it is hid from the eyes of all living, and kept close from the fowls of the air.

Chapter 11 ∴ Wisdom and Knowledge

22 Destruction and death say, We have heard the fame thereof with our ears.
23 God understandeth the way thereof, and he knoweth the place thereof.
28 And unto man he said, Behold, the fear of the Lord, that is wisdom; and to depart from evil is understanding.

Solomon asked for a "hearing heart" which is the literal translation of an understanding mind. When we seek God, who is the source of all wisdom, then we will also gain understanding and knowledge.

1 Kings 3:9 ESV
9 Give your servant therefore an understanding mind to govern your people, that I may discern between good and evil, for who is able to govern this your great people?

KNOWLEDGE

We normally consider that wisdom is knowledge applied and that is probably true in terms of earthly wisdom. But the biblical perspective of wisdom is that it comes first and then knowledge is knowing what to do or how to go in the door.

Ecclesiastes 8:5-6 KJV
5 Whoso keepeth the commandment shall feel no evil thing: and a wise man's heart discerneth both time and judgment.
6 Because to every purpose there is time and judgment, therefore the misery of man is great upon him.

For everything we do, there is a proper time and a procedure. You need both in order to have wisdom. If you have the right procedure but perform it at the wrong time, great is your misery. In every situation and every relationship, this principle holds true. There is a proper time and a proper judgment, and both come from God as the source.

Chapter 11 ∴ Wisdom and Knowledge

There are two wonderful verses in Isaiah that talk about wisdom and knowledge being the stability of the times.

> *Isaiah 33:5-6 NIV*
> *5 The LORD is exalted, for he dwells on high; he will fill Zion with his justice and righteousness.*
> *6 He will be the sure foundation for your times, a rich store of salvation and wisdom and knowledge; the fear of the LORD is the key to this treasure.*

God is the stability, the sure foundation of your times, if you go to him reverently as the source. He is the source of wisdom and knowledge. He is our foundation for living.

It is available to walk worthy of the calling of God, to walk in balance. We must have a balance in all areas of our lives: wisdom and knowledge, Spirit and truth. What connects and enables the balance of all of these is spiritual understanding. We cannot always know what to do by our five senses, but we can humbly go to God, ask, listen, look and cry aloud for spiritual understanding to apply wisdom and knowledge. The beginning of wisdom and knowledge starts with God. As we go to him in humility, searching for spiritual understanding, we will know what to say, how to perform it at the right time and how to apply it so that wisdom can guide our lives. We have doctrine and practice, wisdom and knowledge. The key to it all is spiritual understanding.

Chapter 12 ❖ Walk by Faith

In various teachings over the years, I have called our walk by faith or believing as "faithing." That is because in English we do not have a verb that corresponds to faith as a noun. In many other languages, the noun is built from a similar verbal root. In German, for example, the word for faith is *glaube* and to believe is *glauben*. That is true for Hebrew, Aramaic and Greek also.

> *Romans 1:16-17 APNT*
> *16 For I am not ashamed of the gospel, because it is the power of God for the life of all who believe in it, whether [they are] from the Judeans first or from the heathens.*
> *17 For the uprightness of God is revealed in it from faith to faith, as it is written: The upright [one] will live by faith.*

The gospel reveals the power of God for life. It is not only for our initial salvation, but it should be evident in our entire lives. The uprightness or righteousness of God is revealed from the beginning of faith to the end of faith. Faith is to continue throughout our whole lives. We live always by faith.

The Hebrew word for faith is *aman* and the Aramaic is *emen*, which is very similar. Let's take a look at the word picture.

Seed – water – ox (meaning strength or strong one)

The word picture is **the strong water to the seed**. Seed also represents life. A seed needs the best water in order to grow. To believe means to allow the water to saturate the seed and cause it to grow. Faith will grow when it is watered.

The action of the verb means to "lean or stand on for support." The basic idea is firmness or certainty, as in the strong arms of a parent supporting a child. This is seen in the derivative nouns and adjectives of *aman*: faithfulness, amen, firmness, fidelity, verily, indeed, truth, support, nurture, pillar, believer (one who stands firmly on God's Word).

The first use in the Bible of the Hebrew word *aman* is about Abraham.

> *Genesis 15:6 NET*
> *Abram believed [aman] the LORD, and the LORD considered his response of faith as proof of genuine loyalty.*

God counted righteousness to Abraham because after he heard the promise that he would be the father of many nations, he kept "watering" the promise. He based his certainty on God's promise and his faith grew. His response of faith was counted as righteousness to him. We should "walk in the steps of the faith of our father Abraham" (Romans 4:12) and lean on God's promises.

The first place the Hebrew noun *emunah* is used is in the record of the children of Israel and their war with the Amalekites. As long as Moses held up his staff, they were winning. But eventually, Aaron and Hur came to hold up his hands.

> *Exodus 17:12 KJV*
> *But Moses' hands were heavy; and they took a stone, and put it under him, and he sat thereon; and Aaron and Hur stayed up his hands, the one on the one side, and the other on the other side; and his hands were steady [emunah] until the going down of the sun.*

This shows that there is a certainty or sureness about faith.

> *Romans 10:8-11 APNT*
> *8 But what does it say? The answer is near to you, to your mouth and to your heart, which is the word of faith that we preach.*

Chapter 12 ∴ Walk by Faith

9 And if you confess with your mouth our Lord Jesus and you believe in your heart that God raised him from the dead, you will have life.
10 For the heart that believes in him is justified and the mouth that confesses him has life.
11 For the scripture said: All who believe in him will not be ashamed.

Then, what we put in our mind with certainty comes out of our mouth and heart. Faith also comes by obedience to what we hear.

Romans 10:17 ESV
So faith comes from hearing, and hearing through the word of Christ.

The Eastern idea of hearing is quite a bit different than ours. Hearing implies an obedient action in response to what is heard. "Listening, in our culture, is a passive mental activity, and hearing just means that our ears registered sound waves. But in Hebrew, the word *shema* (to hear) describes hearing and also its outward effects of taking heed, being obedient, and doing what is asked."[22] And this hearing is by the word of or regarding Christ. Many texts read "the word of God" but since the whole Bible is really about Christ, it is that on which our faith is based. Faith has an object and the object of Christian faith is Christ. A fellow minister, Steve Hartlaub, puts it very succinctly: "The obedience of faith is to walk in the revelation of the Christ within, which is to walk in the reality of what the spirit of God has taught you and is teaching you."[23] As we walk in faith and obedience, faith grows!

Let's look at a record about Hannah to see how she "watered" the words that Eli spoke to her. Hannah's husband Elkanah loved her and favored her above his other wife, Penninah. But Penninah had children and Hannah was barren, so she was very grieved by the taunting of this other wife. This went on for years, but one year when they were worshipping the Lord in Shiloh, Hannah spoke with Eli the high priest at the time.

---

[22] www.pathofobedience.com/words/shama/
[23] Steve Hartlaub, *Give Me Christ*, p. 113.

Chapter 12 ∵ Walk by Faith

1 Samuel 1:9-18 ESV
9 After they had eaten and drunk in Shiloh, Hannah rose. Now Eli the priest was sitting on the seat beside the doorpost of the temple of the LORD.
10 She was deeply distressed and prayed to the LORD and wept bitterly.
11 And she vowed a vow and said, "O LORD of hosts, if you will indeed look on the affliction of your servant and remember me and not forget your servant, but will give to your servant a son, then I will give him to the LORD all the days of his life, and no razor shall touch his head."
12 As she continued praying before the LORD, Eli observed her mouth.
13 Hannah was speaking in her heart; only her lips moved, and her voice was not heard. Therefore Eli took her to be a drunken woman.
14 And Eli said to her, "How long will you go on being drunk? Put your wine away from you."
15 But Hannah answered, "No, my lord, I am a woman troubled in spirit. I have drunk neither wine nor strong drink, but I have been pouring out my soul before the LORD.
16 Do not regard your servant as a worthless woman, for all along I have been speaking out of my great anxiety and vexation."
17 Then Eli answered, "Go in peace, and the God of Israel grant your petition that you have made to him."
18 And she said, "Let your servant find favor in your eyes." Then the woman went her way and ate, and her face was no longer sad.

Eli spoke words to her which she put in her heart and believed. Very shortly afterwards, she conceived Samuel and did end up dedicating him to the Lord. Hannah held with certainty and assurance that what Eli said would come to pass. When she heard the words, she did not see it yet, but that's when the "water" of the word caused her life to change.

This is also where hope comes in to be combined with faith.

Chapter 12 ∵ Walk by Faith

Hebrews 11:1 APNT
Now faith is the persuasion concerning those [things] that are in hope,
as if they had in fact happened, and the evidence of those [things] that
are not seen.

Hebrews 11:1 NET
Now faith is being sure of what we hope for, being convinced of what we
do not see.

Faith is the persuasion concerning things that have not yet come to pass,
as though they had already happened. And it is a surety in one's heart.
Faithing or believing is being convinced that what God has promised, he
will bring to pass.

Romans 4:16-21 NLT
16 So the promise is received by faith. It is given as a free gift. And we
are all certain to receive it, whether or not we live according to the law
of Moses, if we have faith like Abraham's. For Abraham is the father of
all who believe.
17 That is what the Scriptures mean when God told him, "I have made
you the father of many nations." This happened because Abraham
believed in the God who brings the dead back to life and who creates
new things out of nothing.
18 Even when there was no reason for hope, Abraham kept hoping –
believing that he would become the father of many nations. For God had
said to him, "That's how many descendants you will have!"
19 And Abraham's faith did not weaken, even though, at about 100
years of age, he figured his body was as good as dead – and so was
Sarah's womb.
20 Abraham never wavered in believing God's promise. In fact, his faith
grew stronger, and in this he brought glory to God.
21 He was fully convinced that God is able to do whatever he promises.

Chapter 12 ∴ Walk by Faith

The promise is certain; therefore, Abraham could rest on it. God was the one who would "call into existence the things that do not exist."

In the King James Version, verse 18 shows how Abraham rested on the hope of what God said. The word "on" in Greek is *epi* and can be translated, "resting on." When there was no reason for hope, Abraham kept hoping. Another way this verse could be translated is "without hope he (Abraham) believed, resting on the hope that he would become the father of many nations."

Now I want to look at a few keys to living by faith.

> *Hebrews 10:22-24 APNT*
> *22 Therefore, we should come near with a steadfast heart and with the confidence of faith, our hearts being sprinkled and pure from an evil conscience and our body washed with pure water.*
> *23 And we should persist in the confession of our hope and we should not waver, for he is faithful who promised us.*
> *24 And we should gaze on one another with an encouragement to love and good works.*

The first key is to draw near with a steadfast heart. The object of faith is Christ and therefore we can have confidence. The second key is to persist in the confession of our hope because God is faithful to fulfill his promises. Then we should "provoke" one another with encouragement. As we have been sharing throughout this book, our walk is together and often we need the encouragement of our fellow believers to be able to "water" our faith so it can grow. We are going to talk more about good works in another chapter.

Another key is not to shrink back in fear or discouragement.

Chapter 12 ∴ Walk by Faith

> *Hebrew 10:35-39 APNT*
> *35 Therefore, do not lose the boldness that you have, for it will have a great reward.*
> *36 For endurance is necessary for you to do the will of God and to receive the promise:*
> *37 Because it is a little, even a very short time, that he who comes will come and he will not delay.*
> *38 Now the upright will live by my faith and if he should be discouraged, I will not be pleased with him.*
> *39 But we are not of the drawing back that leads to loss, but of the faith that obtains for us our life.*

Drawing back will lead to loss, but faith will lead to victory and salvation of every kind.

The last key to walking by faith is to lay aside every weight and unfasten all the burdens from us, looking to Jesus as our example and finisher of faith.

> *Hebrews 12:1-2 APNT*
> *1 Because of this also, we, who have all these witnesses that surround us like a cloud, should unfasten all our burdens from us, even the sin that is always prepared for us, and we should run with patience this race that is set for us.*
> *2 And we should look at Jesus, who was the initiator and finisher of our faith, who for the joy there was for him endured the cross and discounted the shame and sat down at the right hand of the throne of God.*

The just one will live by faith, from the beginning of faith to the end of faith. Let us continue to apply these keys and "water the seed" with the promises of God for HE IS FAITHFUL!

Chapter 13 ❖ Walking in Good Works

We have explored extensively how to walk by the Spirit and that this should be our lifestyle. Now I want to talk about walking in the good works that God has prepared for us and how to be zealous to do that.

> *1 Corinthians 14:12 KJV*
> *Even so ye, forasmuch as ye are zealous of spiritual gifts, seek that ye may excel to the edifying of the church.*

The word "gifts" is in italics in the King James Version, so it means it was added by the translators. It should read spiritual matters or things, but what things? In this chapter, it is talking about the manifestations of the Spirit, but especially prophecy.

We are to seek to excel – exceed, abound or overflow. When I was visiting my grandchildren, Samuel was practicing throwing a football. He threw it over and over and as he practiced, he was getting better and better at both throwing and catching the football. When we seek to excel in something, it takes practice and concerted effort.

We are to abound to the edifying or building up of the church. Another activity that my grandchildren love to do is to build with Legos. They have designed all kinds of houses, complete with kitchens, bedrooms, garages and even with farms surrounding them. Building does not take just a moment; it requires concerted effort, planning and execution.

> *Titus 2:14 APNT*
> *who gave himself for us, so that he could deliver us from all wickedness and would purify for himself a new people who are zealous in good works.*

Zealous means "totally committed" as it is translated in the New Living Translation. Zeal has focus and it is uncompromising – radical! It is like a laser beam. We are to be focused on good works. Now what are these works?

> *Ephesians 2:10 APNT*
> *For we [are] his own creation, who are created in Jesus Christ for good works, those [works] which God prepared previously that we should walk in.*

There are personal works that God has prepared as well as works for all his children, such as the manifestations of the Spirit. These are always GOOD works and God actually prepares the works for us to walk in. We don't have to manufacture them. Sometimes people err when they put too much emphasis on who we are in Christ and think that "works" is a dirty word. Actually, works are the testimony of our faith. People can see our works and glorify God because they come from him.

> *James 2:18 APNT*
> *For a man will say to you, "You have faith," and to me, "I have works." Show me your faith without works and I will show you my faith by my works.*

So what are some works that every believer should be zealous of?

PRAYER

> *Colossians 4:12-13 APNT*
> *12 Epaphras greets you, who is one of you, a servant of Christ, laboring at all times for you in prayer, that you would stand, mature [ones] and complete [ones] in all the will of God.*
> *13 For I witness about him that he has great zeal for you and for those who are in Laodicea and in Hierapolis.*

Epaphras was a great example of a minister who had prayer at the top of the list of works. His prayers were that the believers in Colossae and the surrounding areas would be able to stand and become mature. We will talk more about how to make prayer a lifestyle in chapter 19.

GIVING

> *2 Corinthians 9:1-2 APNT*
> *1 Now concerning the service of the holy [ones], it would be excessive if I wrote to you.*
> *2 For I know the goodness of your mind and because of this, I boasted of you to the Macedonians that Achaia was ready a year ago and your zeal has excited many.*

Corinth is in Achaia (Greece) and their zeal for giving was used by Paul as an example. The New Living Translation version makes this clearer.

> *2 Corinthians 9:2 NLT*
> *For I know how eager you are to help, and I have been boasting to the churches in Macedonia that you in Greece were ready to send an offering a year ago. In fact, it was your enthusiasm that stirred up many of the Macedonian believers to begin giving.*

This kind of zeal is enthusiasm, eagerness [to give], and also stirs up others to give. When we honor God with the firstfruits of our increase (Proverbs 3:9), we are acknowledging that everything we have has come from God to begin with. I read a post recently that God is the first mover and we are the first responders. We form a partnership with him. We purpose in our hearts to respond to God's goodness and love with giving. I think that is such a beautiful way to think about giving.

THANKSGIVING

Along with giving, we can practice thanksgiving with zeal.

Chapter 13 ∴ Walking in Good Works

2 Corinthians 9:10-15 APNT
10 Now he who gives seed to the sower and bread for food will give and will multiply your seed and will increase the fruit of your justification,
11 so that you may be enriched in everything in all simplicity, so that thanksgiving to God is completed by way of us,
12 because the work of this service not only supplies the needs of the holy [ones], but also increases with much thanksgiving to God.
13 For on account of the trial of this service, we glorify God that you have subjected yourselves to the acknowledgment of the gospel of Christ and [that] you have shared fully in your simplicity with them and with everyone.
14 And they offer prayer for you with great love, because of the abundance of the grace of God that is concerning you.
15 Now thanks be to God for his unspeakable gift.

There is much overlap in these various works, so as we can begin to see, these are not isolated works, but go together in the lifestyle of a believer.

Colossians 4:2 APNT
Be steadfast in prayer and be vigilant in it and give thanks.

ACTS OF SERVICE

Romans 12:1-2 APNT
1 Therefore, I beg you, my brothers, by the mercies of God, to present your bodies a living and holy and acceptable sacrifice to God in reasonable service.
2 And do not imitate this world, but be turned the other way by the renewal of your minds and distinguish what is the good and acceptable and perfect will of God.

Chapter 13 ∴ Walking in Good Works

This passage shows how to determine the personal works that God has prepared for us. We present ourselves as willing to do the service and God shows us the specifics.

There is a passage in Romans that has quite a list of types of service.

> Romans 12:10-21 APNT
> 10 Be compassionate to your brothers and love one another. Prefer one another in honor.
> 11 Be diligent and not lazy. Be fervent in spirit. Labor for your Lord.
> 12 Rejoice in your hope. Endure your trials. Be steadfast in prayer.
> 13 Share toward the need of the holy [ones]. Be compassionate [to] strangers.
> 14 Bless your persecutors. Bless and do not curse.
> 15 Rejoice with [those] who are rejoicing and weep with [those] who are weeping.
> 16 And what you think about yourself, also [think] about your brothers. And do not think [with] a proud mind, but associate with those who are meek. And do not be wise in your own mind.
> 17 And do not repay anyone evil [things] for evil [things], but be diligent to do good [things] before all men.
> 18 And if it is possible, according to what is in you, be at peace with everyone.
> 19 And do not avenge yourselves, my beloved, but give place to anger, for it is written: If you will not perform judgment for yourself, I will perform your judgment, says God.
> 20 And if your enemy is hungry, feed him and if he is thirsty, give him drink and if you do these [things] to him, you will heap coals of fire on his head.
> 21 Do not let evil [things] overcome you, but overcome evil [things] with good [things].

Verse 20 is taken from Proverbs 25:21-22 and is to be understood in the same way as Christ directs in Matthew 5:44 about loving your enemies.

Chapter 13 ∴ Walking in Good Works

Jesus instructs his disciples to feed them when they are hungry, and give drink to them when they are thirsty.

In so doing, you will "heap coals of fire on his head," not to do him harm, not to aggravate his condemnation, but by kindness and good things, the evil will be overcome. The Eastern orientalism is of providing coals for a person's fire. It would be easy to do that for a friend, but what about an enemy? The second consequence of treating enemies with kindness is that the Lord will reward the act.

PRAISE AND WORSHIP

> *Hebrews 13:15 APNT*
> *And by way of him, we should always offer up the sacrifices of praise to God, which is the fruit of lips that give thanks to his name.*

In his book called *The Walk*, Adam Hamilton describes worship as follows:

> Worship was not something believers attended. It was not something they watched. It was something they did. They did not gather to be entertained, but to respond to God's love and grace with praise and gratitude, offering themselves to God and seeking to bless others.[24]

Worship can be individual, but it is also in community where praise and honor to God wells up inside and there is great thanksgiving in unity. We will discuss more about praise in the final chapter.

> *Ephesians 5:19-20 APNT*
> *19 and speak among yourselves with psalms and with hymns. And sing in your hearts to the LORD with songs of the Spirit.*

---

[24] Adam Hamilton, *The Walk*, p. 25.

Chapter 13 ∴ Walking in Good Works

20 And give thanks always for everyone in the name of our Lord Jesus Christ to God the Father.

These are just a few of the works that we can be zealous of, but they offer much food for thought about how to apply these things in our individual lives.

We have talked a lot about how to find the path of our journey and about how to walk on it. I wanted to share a little about how I even started being interested in Aramaic to show that this walk truly is a journey and we don't always know how it will progress. In 1978, I took an introductory class in Aramaic from a wonderful woman who had studied with Dr. George Lamsa. It was only about two weeks long, enough to begin to learn how to read the letters and learn a little grammar. I got so excited about the language because to me it painted pictures and was very easy to understand. I knew a little Hebrew, so it was intriguing that this was a cognate (sister) language to the one in the Old Testament. I wanted to learn more, so I asked my teacher if there was any way I could follow up with the class. It opened up for me to study with her for three months and then I was hooked! There were not many books or materials available at that time to study, so she made xerox copies for me of Murdock's translation (those were the days before the Internet) and I had one lexicon. Anyway, little did I know that I would end up teaching classes and making this my life's work.

It definitely was not on my radar at that time to do a whole translation of the New Testament. However, God has such a gentle way of leading and guiding us to accomplish HIS works. As the first computers came out in 1990 (with a 40 mg floppy disk), I started to try to put some of the things I had learned on the computer. Many years and trials later, the database came together as the capacity for work on the computer increased. The point is that the journey unfolded as time went along. If someone had told me I would do some of these things at an earlier time, I would have said that they were not possible. However, God had a different idea and all I did was continue to say, "Yes!" That's all any of us need to do in our lives as we are nudged along the path.

Remember Proverbs 3:5 and 6, "Trust in the LORD with all your heart, and do not lean on your own understanding. In all your ways acknowledge him, and he will make straight your paths." Let's encourage one another, no matter how old or young we are, to continue to respond with agreement to God's direction and guidance.

> *Hebrews 10:24-25 ESV*
> *24 And let us consider how to stir up one another to love and good works,*
> *25 not neglecting to meet together, as is the habit of some, but encouraging one another, and all the more as you see the Day drawing near.*

Chapter 14 ❖ Walk in Newness of Life

God has declared that in Christ we are a new creation and old things have passed away.

> *2 Corinthians 5:17 ESV*
> *Therefore, if anyone is in Christ, he is a new creation. The old has passed away; behold, the new has come.*

When we were born again (born from above), we were given a new life, a spiritual life.

> *Titus 3:4-6 APNT*
> *4 But when the kindness and compassion of God, our Life-giver, was revealed,*
> *5 not by works of justification that we did, but by his own mercies, he gave us life by the washing of the birth from above and by the renewing of the Holy Spirit,*
> *6 which he poured out on us abundantly by way of Jesus Christ, our Life-giver,*

It was by God's mercy that he gave us life when we deserved death. And this is poured out on us! This new life is called different things in the New Testament: the new man (Ephesians 4:24; Colossians 3:10), the inward man (Romans 7:22), a new creation (2 Corinthians 5:17), the hidden man of the heart (1 Peter 3:4) and the spiritual man (1 Corinthians 2:15).

> *Colossians 3:10-11 APNT*
> *10 and put on the new [man] that is renewed in knowledge in the likeness of his Creator,*
> *11 where there is not Judean and Aramean, not circumcision and uncircumcision, not Greek and barbarian, not servant and free[men], but Christ is all and in all men.*

Chapter 14 ∴ Walk in Newness of Life

This new man is the fullness of all Christ is IN us. It is the likeness of the Creator, who is Spirit and who is Holy.

> *Ephesians 4:24 KJV*
> *And that ye put on the new man, which after God is created in righteousness and true holiness.*

If the new man was created, then it had not already existed. It is not a spark of the divine that is fanned into a flame. No one is born with this new nature. A man is made alive when he is born from above. It is as though he is raised from the dead as Christ was.

> *Romans 6:3-5 APNT*
> *3 Or do you not know that we who are baptized in Jesus Christ are baptized in his death?*
> *4 We are buried with him in baptism to death, that as Jesus Christ rose up from the dead in the glory of his Father, so we will also walk in new life.*
> *5 For if we were planted together with him in the likeness of his death, so we will also be in [the likeness of] his resurrection.*

In this "co-resurrection," as Ruth Paxson calls it,[25] God created the new man and opened the way for him to walk in newness of life. We can see further how to walk in this new life with the imagery of being planted. Planted together could be translated "united together" or "implanted." We have been implanted with the resurrection life of Christ.

> *Romans 6:6-11 APNT*
> *6 For we know that our old man was crucified with him that the body of sin should be annulled, so that we should no longer serve sin.*
> *7 For he who is dead is set free from sin.*
> *8 If then we are dead with Christ, we should believe that we will live with Christ.*

---

[25] Ruth Paxson, *The Wealth, Walk and Warfare of the Christian*, p. 111.

9 For we know that Christ rose up from the dead and will not die again and death does not have authority over him.
10 For in dying, he died to sin one time, and in living, he lives to God.
11 So also you should count yourselves that you are dead to sin and alive to God in our Lord Jesus Christ.

In order to walk in new life, we need to understand that the old life was crucified with Christ also. And just as Jesus was buried in the grave, we need to count that our old manner of living is dead and buried with him.

To "put on the new man" will mean an eager seeking after spiritual riches and setting our thoughts and desires on heavenly things, rather than earthly things.

Colossians 3:1-4 APNT
1 Therefore, if you have risen with Christ, seek what is above, where Christ sits at the right hand of God.
2 Think what is above and not what is on the earth,
3 for you are dead and your life is hidden with Christ in God.
4 And when Christ, who is our life, is revealed, then you also will be revealed with him in glory.

Colossians goes on to show some very specific things to do and uses the term "put off" and "put on" as we put on clothes. We have been clothed with the new man. Now we need to put that nature on in our minds and in our actions and strip off the old habits and manner of living.

Colossians 3:5-9 NLT
5 So put to death the sinful, earthly things lurking within you. Have nothing to do with sexual immorality, impurity, lust, and evil desires. Don't be greedy, for a greedy person is an idolater, worshiping the things of this world.
6 Because of these sins, the anger of God is coming.
7 You used to do these things when your life was still part of this world.

8 But now is the time to get rid of anger, rage, malicious behavior, slander, and dirty language.
9 Don't lie to each other, for you have stripped off your old sinful nature and all its wicked deeds.

Ephesians explains what we are to put off. We are going to read this section from the New Living Translation, but not in order. Look at the things to put off first, and then what to put on.

Ephesians 4:25-31 NLT
25 So stop telling lies. Let us tell our neighbors the truth, for we are all parts of the same body.
26 And "don't sin by letting anger control you." Don't let the sun go down while you are still angry,
27 for anger gives a foothold to the devil.
28 If you are a thief, quit stealing. Instead, use your hands for good hard work, and then give generously to others in need.
29 Don't use foul or abusive language. Let everything you say be good and helpful, so that your words will be an encouragement to those who hear them.
30 And do not bring sorrow to God's Holy Spirit by the way you live. Remember, he has identified you as his own, guaranteeing that you will be saved on the day of redemption.
31 Get rid of all bitterness, rage, anger, harsh words, and slander, as well as all types of evil behavior.

Ephesians 4:21-24 NLT
21 Since you have heard about Jesus and have learned the truth that comes from him,
22 throw off your old sinful nature and your former way of life, which is corrupted by lust and deception.
23 Instead, let the Spirit renew your thoughts and attitudes.
24 Put on your new nature, created to be like God — truly righteous and holy.

Chapter 14 ∵ Walk in Newness of Life

Ephesians 4:32-5:2 NLT
32 Instead, be kind to each other, tenderhearted, forgiving one another,
just as God through Christ has forgiven you.
1 Imitate God, therefore, in everything you do, because you are his dear
children.
2 Live a life filled with love, following the example of Christ. He loved
us and offered himself as a sacrifice for us, a pleasing aroma to God.

The walk in newness of life requires a radical change in character (what we are), in conduct (what we do), in conversation (what we say), and in our thoughts (what we think). We read the beginning of Colossians 3 earlier, but it continues on to define more specifically what this new walk looks like.

Colossians 3:10-17 NLT
10 Put on your new nature, and be renewed as you learn to know your
Creator and become like him.
11 In this new life, it doesn't matter if you are a Jew or a Gentile,
circumcised or uncircumcised, barbaric, uncivilized, slave, or free.
Christ is all that matters, and he lives in all of us.
12 Since God chose you to be the holy people he loves, you must clothe
yourselves with tenderhearted mercy, kindness, humility, gentleness, and
patience.
13 Make allowance for each other's faults, and forgive anyone who
offends you. Remember, the Lord forgave you, so you must forgive
others.
14 Above all, clothe yourselves with love, which binds us all together in
perfect harmony.
15 And let the peace that comes from Christ rule in your hearts. For as
members of one body you are called to live in peace. And always be
thankful.
16 Let the message about Christ, in all its richness, fill your lives.
Teach and counsel each other with all the wisdom he gives. Sing psalms
and hymns and spiritual songs to God with thankful hearts.

Chapter 14 ∴ Walk in Newness of Life

17 And whatever you do or say, do it as a representative of the Lord Jesus, giving thanks through him to God the Father.

I know there have been a lot of scriptures in this chapter, but instead of expounding on each verse, I wanted them to speak to each person's individual heart. We can each learn something from these verses about what to put off and what to put on. We are to grow up into Christ and be "a representative of the Lord Jesus." He is our example of how to love and walk as an imitator of the Father God. He exhibited all the qualities of kindness, humility and forgiveness that are in the above verses. Let us endeavor to walk as he walked. Murdock has a beautiful translation that describes the simplicity of our walk in Christ.

1 John 2:6 MRD
He that saith, I am in him, is bound to walk according to his walkings.

Chapter 15 ❖ What's Your Excuse?

The next few chapters are going to share practical insight into how to follow Jesus' example and walk as he walked.

Selfishness is THE major reason why believers do not follow Jesus and do not end up accomplishing the fulfillment of their ministries and service to the Lord. That may be a pretty harsh thing to say to start a chapter, but IT IS TRUE. There are different ways that selfishness manifests itself in people's lives. These are the excuses that we all use at one time or another for not following him. I want to look at them one at a time and see the application to our culture. This chapter will be confronting, but prayerfully, it will show us (me, too) how to avoid these pitfalls.

Rather than starting with the negative, I want to first read the response that Simon Peter, Andrew, James and John had when Jesus called them to become fishermen of men.

> *Mark 1:16-18 APNT*
> *16 And while walking round about the Sea of Galilee, he saw Simon and Andrew, his brother, who were casting nets into the sea, for they were fishermen.*
> *17 And Jesus said to them, "Follow me and I will make you fishermen of men."*
> *18 And immediately they left their nets and followed him.*

When Jesus said to them, "Follow me," it says immediately they left their nets and followed him. Sometimes in different contexts, we are to count the cost of something before directly plunging in, as for example, in going to war with a neighbor. It's not a good idea to just dive in and then find out that your neighbor has an army of 100,000 to your 2,000. But in this case, the four fishermen did not hesitate in any way. They left their nets and followed him. Did they know that James would suffer a martyr's death, or that they would travel and go through much persecution? They had NO idea what it would mean to follow him. If they had, perhaps they would not have been so eager to leave their nets! Did they know that they would see miracle after miracle, or that they would themselves learn how to walk with power and be witnesses of the resurrection? Not hardly. They grew into the experience of all of that. It was enough at the moment that Jesus called them to just respond with a wholehearted willingness to follow. That is really all he ever asks us to do. What are the various excuses that we make not to follow or come to him?

The following is a list of excuses. I will not say these are the only ones, but they are certainly a good place to start to take a mental inventory of our own lives. Please take the time to read the passages to get the full impact of the records.

1. Too busy (with other priorities)
2. Distracted or burdened by riches
3. Wrong motivation
4. But first...
5. Looking at others

TOO BUSY

> *Luke 14:16-21 APNT*
> *16 Jesus said to him, "A certain man made a great supper and called many.*
> *17 And he sent his servant at the time of the supper to tell those who were called, 'Behold, everything is prepared for you. Come.'*
> *18 And all began as one to excuse themselves. The first said to him, 'I have bought a field and I need to go out [and] see it. I beg you, allow me to be excused.'*
> *19 Another said, 'I have bought five yoke [of] oxen and I am going to prove them. I beg you, allow me to be excused.'*

20 And another said, 'I have taken a wife and because of this, I am not able to come.'
21 And that servant came and told his lord these [things]. Then the lord of the house was angry and said to his servant, 'Go out quickly into the marketplaces and streets of the city and bring here the poor and the afflicted and the lame and the blind.'

In this parable, there are three people who "began as one to excuse themselves" from the invitation to the feast. Their excuses were that they had some other more important things to do. They were too busy. The first one said that he had bought a field and needed to go out and see it. The second person said that he had bought five pair of oxen and needed to "prove" them, which means not only to examine them, but also to test them out. The third person said that he had just taken a wife and because it was customary to spend at least a year on a honeymoon, it was not possible for him to come. These excuses were valid things that these people were doing. The point of the parable is that they put these things above the invitation. Their priorities were to be busy about their own business and not to consider anything else. What is important to you? This will always set the priorities of what you do.

DISTRACTED OR BURDENED BY RICHES

Matthew 19:16-24 APNT
16 And a certain [man] came [and] approached and said to him, "Good teacher, what good [thing] should I do that I might have eternal life?"
17 Now he said to him, "Why do you call me good? There is no good [one], except one, God. Now if you want to enter life, keep the commandments."
18 He said to him, "Which [ones]?" And Jesus said to him, "Do not kill and do not commit adultery and do not steal and do not give false testimony.
19 And honor your father and your mother and love your neighbor as yourself."

Chapter 15 ∴ What's Your Excuse?

20 That young man said to him, "All these [things] I have kept from my youth. What do I lack?"
21 Jesus said to him, "If you want to be mature, go, sell your possessions and give [them] to the poor and you will have treasure in heaven and follow me."
22 And that young man heard this word and went away, feeling sorry for himself, for he had many possessions.
23 Now Jesus said to his disciples, "Truly I say to you, it is difficult for a rich man to enter into the kingdom of heaven.
24 And again I say to you, it is easier for a camel to enter into the eye of a needle than [for] a rich man to enter into the kingdom of God."

This man had come to ask Jesus what he must do to have eternal life. He had been keeping the commandments, so that was not an issue. But then Jesus told him to sell his possessions and give to the poor. Ouch! It hit his pocketbook and he went away very sad, because he had many possessions. The riches were burdening him down and had a hold on him. That is why he did not want to let them go. Both riches and debt can have this effect. They cause us to be distracted and burdened and to focus all our time and energy on either obtaining them or getting rid of them.

An opposite example of a disciple who was not burdened or distracted by his wealth was the tax collector, Matthew. Matthew 9:9 says that he was sitting at the seat of the customs-house when Jesus called him to follow him. He was very likely making a lot of money. But he arose and followed him. Simple, just like that, without a lot of agony or consideration of what it would mean financially. That's why I know that his wealth was not controlling him. Does wealth or debt control your life in any way?

Chapter 15 ∴ What's Your Excuse?

WRONG MOTIVATION

> *Luke 9:57-58 APNT*
> *57 And while they were traveling on the road, a man said to him, "I will follow you wherever you go, my Lord."*
> *58 Jesus said to him, "Foxes have holes and a bird of heaven a shelter, but the Son of Man has no where to lay his head."*

Jesus responded to the man with a proverb that simply meant that he did not have a permanent dwelling or house to call his own. The reason he said this is that the man wanted to follow Jesus so that he could be taken care of. It appears at first that the man wanted to follow Jesus. But really, he was not interested in serving or helping or being a disciple, only that he would be provided for. He had a wrong motivation for wanting to follow Jesus. Why do you want to serve the Lord? For recognition? To have a job?

BUT FIRST...

In the next verses in that same chapter of Luke, Jesus calls two others to follow him. Their responses were very similar with the excuse of "but first" in their replies.

> *Luke 9:59-62 APNT*
> *59 And he said to another, "Follow me." And he said to him, "My Lord, allow me first to go [and] bury my father."*
> *60 Jesus said to him, "Leave the dead burying their dead and go [and] preach the kingdom of God."*
> *61 Another said to him, "I will follow you, my Lord, but first allow me to go [and] say goodbye to my household and [then] I will come."*
> *62 Jesus said to him, "No one places his hand on the handle of a plow and looks back and is useful for the kingdom of God."*

Chapter 15 ∴ What's Your Excuse?

The first man said that he needed to go and bury his father. This did not mean that his father was dead already, but that he needed to care for his father into his old age. The second man said that he needed to go to say goodbye to his household. This also meant an extended period of time in household obligations. Remember Jacob? He ended up staying in Haran and working for Laban for more than 21 years before he left. The answer that Jesus gives is also a proverb. "No man places his hand on the handle of a plow and looks backwards and is useful to the kingdom of God." We will look backwards if we think our own ideas are more important than the Lord's. We can recognize this excuse by hearing ourselves say, "but first…"

LOOKING AT OTHERS

> *John 21:19-23 APNT*
> *19 Now he said this to show by what death he would glorify God. And after he had said these [things], he said to him, "Follow me."*
> *20 And Simon Peter turned and saw the disciple whom Jesus loved who followed him, who fell on the breast of Jesus during the supper and said, 'My Lord, who will betray you?'"*
> *21 When Peter saw this [man], he said to Jesus, "My Lord, and what [of] this [man]?"*
> *22 Jesus said to him, "If I desire that this [man] should remain until I come, what is it to you? Follow me."*
> *23 And this saying went out among the brothers that that disciple would not die. But Jesus did not say that he would not die, but rather, "If I desire that this [man] should remain until I come, what is it to you?"*

After the resurrection, Jesus confronted Peter lovingly and told him to "feed my sheep." Peter's only question to Jesus was, "Lord, and what of this man?" referring to another disciple. Jesus told Peter in essence, not to worry about him, just be concerned about yourself and what you are doing – FOLLOW ME. If we look at what other people are doing and compare ourselves with them and then moan about how our lives are not the same and we don't get to do this or that, we have entered into a complaining session. Forget it! Just follow Jesus.

These excuses are very confronting, aren't they? They all point to selfishness of one kind or another. How can we change this? I think that if we put the lessons in the positive, it would be summarized like this:

> *Matthew 16:24-26 APNT*
> *24 Then Jesus said to his disciples, "He who wants to follow me should deny himself and take up his cross and follow me.*
> *25 For he who wants to save his life will lose it. And he who will lose his life because of me will find it.*
> *26 For what does a man profit if he gains the whole world and loses his life? Or what [thing of] exchange will a man give for his life?"*

To deny oneself means to lose sight of one's own self and interests and to put God first. That will set the correct priorities and keep riches or debt from being a burden or distraction. Taking up his cross means to get busy doing the Lord's business. There is no room in there for "me first" or other obligations. To follow the Lord, we must be looking at him and not at other people.

Let us consider these matters prayerfully, so that we can be set free from anything that is holding us back from following him. What's your excuse?

Chapter 16 ❖ Faint Not

What can we do about being discouraged? Galatians 6:9 says, "And let us not be weary in well doing: for in due season we shall reap, if we faint not." Yet so many times, it is difficult to not faint. We cannot prevent getting tired, but we can train our minds so that we can continue to walk the path God has called us to with contentment.

I would like us to consider this chart for our study in this chapter. It shows two sets of opposites, a path down to despair and a path up to contentment.

DISILLUSIONMENT	CONVICTION
DISCOURAGEMENT	CONFIDENCE
DISTRACTION	CONCENTRATION
DESPAIR	CONTENTMENT

On the path down, disillusionment comes when we say things like Isaiah did in Isaiah 49:4 (ESV): But I said, "I have labored in vain; I have spent my strength for nothing and vanity; yet surely my right is with the Lord, and my recompense with my God." The Lord answered him in the following verses that he had set out a plan of salvation for his people and they would also be a light to the Gentiles.

> *Isaiah 49:5-6 ESV*
> *5 And now the LORD says, he who formed me from the womb to be his servant, to bring Jacob back to him; and that Israel might be gathered to him — for I am honored in the eyes of the LORD, and my God has become my strength —*
> *6 he says: "It is too light a thing that you should be my servant to raise up the tribes of Jacob and to bring back the preserved of Israel; I will make you as a light for the nations, that my salvation may reach to the end of the earth."*

Chapter 16 ∴ Faint Not

God set a vision for Isaiah, so that he could see that his life was a part of something much bigger – VISION! The opposite of disillusionment is holding onto a vision of what GOD'S PLAN is for us, for the church, for the whole earth. Our vision gets nearsighted at times, because we are only looking at ourselves and what we may or may not be accomplishing.

David kept his heart on the vision of what God had told him.

> *Psalm 16:8-10 ESV*
> *8 I have set the LORD always before me; because he is at my right hand, I shall not be shaken.*
> *9 Therefore my heart is glad, and my whole being rejoices; my flesh also dwells secure.*
> *10 For you will not abandon my soul to Sheol, or let your holy one see corruption.*

We have the Hope of Christ's return as our greater vision. I believe that God also gives us specific vision for our own lives, so we can hold to that when the going gets tough. To "not be shaken" is conviction. It is conviction that what God said, whether it was in the written Word or in specific revelation or prophecy to you, WILL come to pass. The point is to get our sights up and become farsighted instead of only looking at the present. Conviction is being persuaded that something you believe in is absolute. It is not difficult to be convinced that Jesus is our Savior. We would be hard-pressed to be talked out of that. Then let us hold to the vision of the Hope and not be disillusioned that our life is in vain.

The second step down is discouragement. Without a purpose, working and serving others can be very discouraging. Often there is little acknowledgement of anything that we do. Discouragement means "not courageous." The Christian walk is not for the "cowardly lion" type of people. The cares and riches of the world will quickly choke those out as in the parable of the sower. There are many verses in the Psalms where

Chapter 16 ∴ Faint Not

David confesses that he is looking at the wicked and wondering why it always seems that they prosper and he is surrounded by enemies. God explains that the end of the wicked is certain and it is NOT GOOD. We know that, but sometimes it is still difficult to keep going and not to succumb to a cloud of depression.

The antidote is confidence, or certainty, that God's promises are "yea and amen" (2 Corinthians 1:20) and HE is faithful. In order to have this kind of confidence, we have to keep the promises of God in our minds. In Philippians 4:11, Paul explains, "for I have learned that what I have will be sufficient for me." This passage has the key of confidence that we are discussing.

> *Philippians 4:6-9 APNT*
> *6 Do not be distressed about anything, but at all times, by prayer and by petition and with thanksgiving, your requests should be made known before God.*
> *7 And the peace of God that is greater than all knowledge will guard your hearts and your minds in Jesus Christ.*
> *8 From now on, my brothers, those [things] that are true and those [things] that are modest and those [things] that are upright and those [things] that are pure and those [things] that are lovely and those [things] that are praiseworthy and those works of glory and of commendation, think these [things].*
> *9 Those [things] that you have learned and received and heard and seen in me, these do and the God of peace will be with you.*

I know from painful experience that if I complain about my circumstances, I get discouraged. But when I take the time to read the Word and see how many times God promises that he will provide all my need, I am refreshed and filled with a new confidence. I need to think about the "mini-victories" that happen each and every day because of God's blessings, like when I find something for half-price that was needed, or an unexpected check comes in the mail, or someone reports being healed. Those "good reports" reinforce the confidence that God "will never leave us or forsake us." I can hold to the certainty of the promises of God's Word.

The third step down is distraction, which leads to despair. Discouragement causes us to become distracted from our relationship with God. We can see this in cases of depression, where the person wants to avoid any decisions and perhaps just go to sleep for a while. Not dealing with the problems head-on with concentration and focus will then lead to despair. Distraction means to be diverted away from something. If the Evil One can lead us away from our relationship with our heavenly Father and our Lord, then he has gained the upper hand in the battle.

> Isaiah 40:28-31 ESV
> 28 Have you not known? Have you not heard? The LORD is the everlasting God, the Creator of the ends of the earth. He does not faint or grow weary; his understanding is unsearchable.
> 29 He gives power to the faint, and to him who has no might he increases strength.
> 30 Even youths shall faint and be weary, and young men shall fall exhausted;
> 31 but they who wait for the LORD shall renew their strength; they shall mount up with wings like eagles; they shall run and not be weary; they shall walk and not faint.

The Lord who is the Creator of the earth does not faint! He gives strength to those who are faint. Waiting on the Lord is to continue with him, to abide in his presence, and to FOCUS on him. The antidote to distraction is concentration. But concentration on what? On God as our Father, on the Lord as our Savior and on the promises of God's Word.

Philippians 4:13 is a well-known verse that has brought comfort to many. However, the King James Version is misleading when it says, "I can do all things." The truth of the matter is that many times we cannot do all things and fall very far short of what we know is even available. What then? I think that the Aramaic translation is much clearer here and helps to define the focus on Christ as our sufficiency, not ourselves. The translation is: "I find strength for everything in Christ who strengthens me." We will FIND the strength in every situation in CHRIST. Only in him! This is the same idea as the verse from Isaiah about waiting on the Lord. It is in relationship with God and the Lord Jesus Christ – helping us, giving us revelation, praying, praising, all this and much more – that we find strength. We do not walk alone on the path. We are strengthened in Christ even when situations lead to despair.

Despair is a harsh word that implies coming to the end of your rope. But contentment is a wonderful goal that when realized brings true joy. One of the definitions of contentment in the dictionary is "to be held in." Paul explained to the Philippians what it took to keep this contentment.

> *Philippians 4:11-13 APNT*
> *11 Now I do not say [this] because I am in need, for I have learned that what I have will be sufficient for me.*
> *12 I know [how] to be humble. I also know [how] to abound in every [situation] and I am disciplined in everything, whether in plenty or in famine, in abundance or in need.*
> *13 I find strength for everything in Christ who strengthens me.*

Paul said that he was "disciplined." This is a very interesting word in Aramaic. One of the things I love about studying the Eastern languages is that it paints pictures for me. Very often there is an action root for a word because all words belong in word families. That action root gives me a picture in order to understand something. In this case, the word *darash* has a root picture meaning "to beat a path," or in other words, to practice.

Chapter 16 ∴ Faint Not

My sons Mark and Stephen were involved in sports in high school and their favorite one was volleyball. In their workouts and practices, they "beat a path" over and over with the correct way to jump, hit and set up the ball. When it comes to the game, the path is so ingrained in the player's mind that it is an automatic response. It is the same thing in our Christian walk. If we "beat a path" starting with conviction, confidence and concentration, it WILL bring contentment. It becomes a "training in contentment."

Contentment is not something that comes automatically. It requires perseverance and discipline. We can find the strength in everything as Christ strengthens us. We can hold to the Hope and hope on an ongoing basis and think on all the positives. We can grow in our relationship with our Father and win against the Evil One's plan! We can overcome weariness – walk and not faint. We will reap in due season if we don't faint. That is so encouraging to me and I hope to you, also.

Chapter 17 ❖ Overcoming Worry

"You're just a worry wart!" Did anybody ever call you that? Well, I used to call myself that a lot. Not anymore! Perhaps this may be a simple topic, because I've known for a long time that the Bible says, "Don't be anxious for anything," and "cast all your cares on him," along with many other verses. I don't think that I really understood how to do that before. Not only would the worry crop up, but it would stick, sometimes for days at a time. How do we learn to be worry-free?

Instead of listing some principles and then expecting that you will get the idea, I will share with you in this chapter how I learned more about this topic. I believe that will help you to see the process. Getting rid of worry is a process that we each have to go through in our thinking. If anything gets stopped along the way in the process, then worry remains, to whatever degree. The process is taught in the well-known passage of the Sermon on the Mount. I was studying it in Luke, so this is where we will begin.

> Luke 12:22-32 APNT
> 22 And he said to his disciples, "Because of this, I say to you, do not be anxious for yourselves, what you will eat or for your body, what you will wear,
> 23 for the soul is more than food, and the body than clothes.
> 24 Consider the ravens, for they neither sow nor reap and they do not have rooms and storehouses, yet God provides for them. Therefore, how much more important are you than birds?
> 25 And which of you, being anxious, is able to add one cubit to his stature?
> 26 And if you are not even capable of a small [thing], why are you anxious about the rest?
> 27 Consider how the lilies grow, for they neither labor nor spin, but I say to you, not even Solomon in all his glory was covered as one of these.

Chapter 17 ∴ Overcoming Worry

28 And if God so clothes the grass that today is in the field and
tomorrow falls into the oven, how much more you, [oh] little of faith?
29 And you should not seek what you will eat and what you will drink
and your mind should not wander in these [things].
30 For all these [things] the Gentiles of the world seek. Now your
Father also knows that these [things] are necessary for you.
31 But seek the kingdom of God and all these [things] will be added to
you.
32 Do not fear, little flock, because your Father wants to give you the
kingdom.

Worry is something that can get all bottled up with the business of daily life. There are things that we need to do and decide and figure out every day. Some days the pressures of these decisions are very challenging. The pressure seems to gather momentum. That's when people say things like, "I'm stressed out." Worry comes in when we are stewing about what to do and how to handle things. People react in different ways to this pressure. Some give up and try to avoid the problem and do anything except deal with it. Others get angry and lash out at people around them. Others get depressed and stop talking to anybody. I was one who just let the questions and difficulties go around and around in my thinking, never coming up with any answers.

The first thing that I saw in the passage above was to "consider the ravens." Really consider them for a moment. When you start worrying, consider the ravens. It has become a starting point for me. Ravens are carrion birds that are not very nice. We have crows that come into our backyard, making a big noise, stealing crops and generally being a nuisance. And most of the time, they steal other birds' food. They take the leftovers of a kill by another animal. They are not pretty birds. In fact, in the eastern culture, they were considered unclean, so people did not want to have anything to do with them. Yet, Jesus said, consider the ravens. Why? Because even though they are one of the most unloved birds, God provides for them. He does not think that they are unimportant. They don't have storehouses or work hard to figure out how to save their food; they just have what they need today. The first thing that I realized about the process of getting rid of worry was that I genuinely needed to think that God loved and cared for me and that I was important to him. This goes along with the passage in 1 Peter.

> *1 Peter 5:7 KJV*
> *Casting all your care upon him, for he careth for you.*

The first word for care in this verse is worry or anxiety. The second kind of care is loving compassion. God truly cares for us. Jesus had also said the same basic thing earlier in the sermon in Luke 12.

> *Luke 12:6-8 APNT*
> *6 Are not five birds sold for two coins? And one of them is not forgotten before God.*
> *7 But even the separate hairs of your head are all numbered. Do not fear, therefore, because you are more valuable than a multitude of birds.*
> *8 And I say to you, whoever will confess me before men, the Son of Man also will confess him before the angels of God.*

First, we have to genuinely believe that we are valuable. The next step in the process is brought out in this passage. "Whoever will confess me before men" is the key. What does this mean? It means that we have to stop the confession of the worry. If we can take the worry and put it all in a ball and cast it to God, then we don't have it anymore. Therefore, we can't talk about it. We don't have to cast the whole problem or situation to God, just the worry part. For what will he do with the problem? He can't work it out without us. Many people teach, cast everything to God, for he will take care of you. It doesn't work and they end up taking back the worry, too, when what is needed is to work out the problem.

Chapter 17 ∴ Overcoming Worry

A simple illustration of this happened to me. I had realized that it was very possible that I had not filed a very important IRS form for Light of the Word Ministry. It would have been four months overdue and I could not find any proof anywhere that it had been done. So after the initial flurry of worry, I cast it to God. Then he lovingly told me what to do to find out whether it was indeed an oversight or not. I found the form in good order, so even that initial worry had been unnecessary. Praise God we can continue to grow in this!

The next aspect of this phrase has to do with confession. Remember the Shunamite woman whose son had died? When Gehaza, Elijah's servant, asked how she was, she said, "All is well." Her son had just died! How could she say that all was well? This illustration is not a lesson that we should never confess anything negative that is happening in our lives, for if we do that, the worry just gets more and more buried. It means that we are to confess the problem or need to someone who can help to do something about it. When she came to Elijah, he was able to deal directly with the situation and to restore her son alive and well!

This is a lesson for ministers as well. If people in your charge do confess things that are going on in their lives and problems and needs, it is not for "public consumption." If a person genuinely repents of sins in their lives, these do not need to be broadcast all around the congregation. How will it be possible for the person to overcome their problem if, for example, everyone else knows that they have a severe financial situation or a marital crisis? What good does it do for people to know about it who cannot help? You can say that they could pray. Well, that is true, but even that needs to be done with circumspection, for if the prayers contain more negative worry than positive help, there is not a lot of profit. Or if the prayers contain condemnation of the other person, they are not helpful. And that applies to those intercessors who are truly endeavoring to pray fervently for needs to be met.

Chapter 17 ∴ Overcoming Worry

Once we can cast the "worry" on God, then there is a next step. There is a principle in nature that if you have a void, it must be filled with something. It is not enough to just send the worry away – it must be replaced with something else. This is what "the good portion" is.

> *Luke 10:38-42 APNT*
> *38 And it happened that while they were journeying on the road, he entered a certain village and a woman whose name [was] Martha received him into her house.*
> *39 And she had a sister whose name [was] Mary. And she came [and] seated herself at the feet of our Lord and was listening to his words.*
> *40 But Martha was occupied with much service and came [and] said to him, "My Lord, do you not care that my sister has left me alone to serve? Tell her to help me."*
> *41 But Jesus answered and said to her, "Martha, Martha, you are anxious and troubled about many [things].*
> *42 But there is one [thing] that is necessary and Mary has chosen that good part for herself that will not be taken from her."*

Jesus was not condemning Martha for serving. He was talking to her about the "anxious and troubled" part. And he said that only "one thing is necessary" which is "the good part." Mary chose it in this passage. She was sitting at his feet and LISTENING TO HIS WORDS. What a joy that must have been!

After we cast the worry away, it must be replaced with something. That something is received by coming to sit at Jesus' feet (as it were) and listening to HIS words. It is not coming to ask a lot of questions; it is not coming to complain about why you have this problem. It is coming to LISTEN. We can do this by going to a quiet place to listen to direct revelation and to replace the thoughts of worry with the written Word as well. The key is in being quiet and listening. That is the good portion. Will you choose it?

Chapter 18 ❖ Let Go and Let God

When we are under pressure from health situations or from economic or even political situations, what do we do?

During this past year when things were very stressful, I was learning again about not worrying. God showed me that I kept a "worry bucket" where I put all the worries inside until they seemed to overflow. He reiterated to me that I had to empty the bucket and then actually throw it away. After doing that multiple times, I didn't hold onto my worries anymore, but still didn't know how to handle all the challenges without crumbling.

I let go...but then I had to learn to let God.

> *Proverbs 3:5-6 ESV*
> *5 Trust in the LORD with all your heart, and do not lean on your own understanding.*
> *6 In all your ways acknowledge him, and he will make straight your paths.*

To trust in the Lord is to let go. To lean on...to rely on and acknowledge him are all the letting go part. Then he will straighten your path – make it smooth, show you which way to go or which path to take. That is the "let God" part. The Lord is holding our hands.

> *Psalm 37:23-24 ESV*
> *23 The steps of a man are established by the LORD, when he delights in his way;*
> *24 though he fall, he shall not be cast headlong, for the LORD upholds his hand.*

Now that we understand some of the basic ideas of letting go and letting God, we can take several passages and determine which one the verses are talking about.

Chapter 18 ∴ Let Go and Let God

Psalm 57:1-3 ESV
1 Be merciful to me, O God, be merciful to me, for in you my soul takes refuge; in the shadow of your wings I will take refuge, till the storms of destruction pass by.
2 I cry out to God Most High, to God who fulfills his purpose for me.
3 He will send from heaven and save me; he will put to shame him who tramples on me. Selah. God will send out his steadfast love and his faithfulness!

Let Go	Let God
Take refuge (trust) under his wings (shade of his presence)	Till the storms of destruction pass by
Cry out	He will fulfill his purpose for me (performs all things)
	He will send and save me He will put to shame those who swallow me up (KJV) He will send his love and truth (faithfulness)

I am working on an amplified translation of the Old Testament Peshitta Psalms. Here is the same passage as above.

Psalm 57:1-3
1 Have compassion [mercy] on me, God, for my soul trusts [hopes] in you and in the shadow of your wings I will be concealed [hidden, sheltered, protected] until the trouble [commotion, confusion] be over.
2 I will cry to God Most High, to God my deliverer.
3 For he has sent from heaven and delivered me and he has scorned [put to shame] my enemies. God will send out his grace [goodness] and his truth [faithfulness].

There is another passage to use to build a similar chart.

Chapter 18 ∴ Let Go and Let God

Psalm 37:1-9 ESV
1 Fret not yourself because of evildoers; be not envious of wrongdoers!
2 For they will soon fade like the grass and wither like the green herb.
3 Trust in the LORD, and do good; dwell in the land and befriend
faithfulness.
4 Delight yourself in the LORD, and he will give you the desires of your
heart.
5 Commit your way to the LORD; trust in him, and he will act.
6 He will bring forth your righteousness as the light, and your justice as
the noonday.
7 Be still before the LORD and wait patiently for him; fret not yourself
over the one who prospers in his way, over the man who carries out evil
devices!
8 Refrain from anger, and forsake wrath! Fret not yourself; it tends only
to evil.
9 For the evildoers shall be cut off, but those who wait for the LORD
shall inherit the land.

Let Go	Let God
Do not be envious (fret yourself) because of evildoers	For they will quickly dry up like grass (NET)
Have confidence in the Lord, dwell in the land	You will find safe pasture (NIV) Faithfully you will be fed (KJV)
Delight yourself in the Lord	He will answer the requests of your heart (NET)
Commit your way (roll everything on him)	He will act (on your behalf) (ESV) He will vindicate you in broad daylight, and publicly defend your just cause. (NET)
Be still and wait patiently Refrain from anger and fret not Wait on the Lord	You will inherit the land and enjoy peace (NIV) When the wicked are cut off, you will see it (NASB)

Chapter 18 ∴ Let Go and Let God

We could do a chart like this for many passages with God's promises to us. The point is to remember that when we obey and let go of our own ideas and wait on him, then he will bring the promise to pass. It becomes our armor and protection.

> *Psalm 91:1-4 ESV*
> *1 He who dwells in the shelter of the Most High will abide in the shadow of the Almighty.*
> *2 I will say to the LORD, "My refuge and my fortress, my God, in whom I trust."*
> *3 For he will deliver you from the snare of the fowler and from the deadly pestilence.*
> *4 He will cover you with his pinions (feathers), and under his wings you will find refuge; his faithfulness is a shield and buckler.*

The New Living Translation for verse 4 is "His faithful promises are your armor and protection." We can rely on God's faithfulness!

In the New Testament, there are also many wonderful promises. Here's another "let go, let God."

> *Philippians 4:6-7 ESV*
> *6 do not be anxious about anything, but in everything by prayer and supplication with thanksgiving let your requests be made known to God.*
> *7 And the peace of God, which surpasses all understanding, will guard your hearts and your minds in Christ Jesus.*

Chapter 19 ❖ A Lifestyle of Prayer

As we have seen throughout this book, our life is a walk. In this next to the last chapter, I would like to present how prayer can become a lifestyle.

> *Ephesians 6:18 KJV*
> *Praying always with all prayer and supplication in the Spirit, and watching thereunto with all perseverance and supplication for all saints;*

This verse is right after the section about the armor of God which teaches us to stand against the wiles of the devil. After this, it says to pray always. In the King James Version, there are two places supplication is used, but they mean two different things. It is much clearer in the Aramaic and distinguishes general prayer from petition and intercession (supplication).

> *Ephesians 6:18 APNT*
> *And with all prayers [tselutha] and with all petitions, pray [tsela] at all times spiritually, and in prayer [tselutha], be watchful in every season, praying [tsela] continually and interceding for all the holy [ones]*

The Aramaic word *tsela* is a verb that has a very beautiful word picture. Here are the letters:

$$b\!\!\cdot\!\!J\!a\!\!\wedge$$

aleph – lamed – tzaddi

Remember we need to read the letters from right to left. The tzaddi is a picture of a man on his side and means to hunt or seek. The lamed is the shepherd's staff and can mean what the shepherd does or authority. To me, it is an upside-down staff because we usually have an image in our minds about the crook of the staff on the top. However, I think this staff is very wonderful because it is in action, where the shepherd is using the crook to guide the sheep somewhere. See it? The aleph is the pictograph of an ox and means strong one. So we put these together and the normal verb *tsela*, to pray, means **to seek the shepherding of the strong one**.

Ephesians 6:18 uses the noun and verb of *tsela* in this verse four times. It must be important as the first thing to do after putting on the armor of God! God is the strong one and we are to seek out and hunt for HIS shepherding, not our own ideas. And it explains that this kind of prayer can be done at all times. We can always be seeking the wisdom, guidance and tending of the Lord, our shepherd.

Then it goes on to tell us something else in the rest of the verse, "and watching thereunto with all perseverance and supplication." The "and" connects the verse with the previous passage. Perseverance means consistency, keeping on going. To persevere means that you don't give up. We are supposed to watch without giving up. This supplication here means intercession. We're supposed to make intercession for all the saints. That is why it is so important. The armor of God is so great because it is everything that God gave us in Christ Jesus. He put Christ in us, he gave us the gift of the Spirit, and he gave us power to stand against the Evil One in every situation. We are to continually watch and make intercession for all the saints. It must be important to know what intercession is.

The first element of intercession is to watch, or to keep our eyes open. When we watch or observe then we see things that need to be prayed for. If we don't watch, then we will not know how to begin to make intercession. If I have my head buried in the sand and all I see are things in my life and what is wrong with me and my needs, then I'm like an ostrich and I can't see what others need. But if I have my head up, then I'm putting my eyes where I can be observant of others' needs, and I will see things that need prayer. Everyone needs prayer. And if we are watchful, we'll see plenty of things that need intercession. And God will show us where to focus our attention in prayer.

The second thing is to understand what the word intercession means. Intercession comes from two Latin words: "inter" which means between and "cession" which means to move. It means to move between. The Aramaic word is *palal*. Here are the ancient letters:

ᒐᒐᓄ

lamed – lamed – pey

The pey is an open mouth and mean what the mouth does, which is to speak. The lamed we saw before and it means the shepherd's staff, or authority of the shepherd. When there are two of the same letters together, they form a superlative, and in this case, it means the greatest authority. Putting this together, the simple word picture for *palal* is **to speak to the greatest authority**.

Who is the greatest authority? THE SHEPHERD, God, and the Lord Jesus Christ. We speak to God on behalf of someone else, so we are moving between the person who has a need and God. The action for *palal* is to "meet or go between." We meet with God to entreat or ask him for something specific for the person.

An example is someone who is a soldier. The enemy is over there and I'm in the soldiers' camp. I have a sword in my hand, which is the revelation from God, the sword of the Spirit. Now here comes another believer in the family of Christ and the enemy is attacking them. I move between my brother in Christ and God and entreat God for revelation of what to do in this situation and for him to go to battle. It is not that I just decide to go stand between the enemy and this person and be the buffer because that would be prideful. It is not that I believe that I am great enough or have enough strength or know how to be a buffer. But I can do it because I have my armor on and especially because I have revelation. Then God can tell me to stand right there, right where the enemy is attacking. That revelation will direct the intercession.

Another example is that the enemy is coming for you and by revelation God can show me to warn you and say, "Hey watch out on the right! Here comes the enemy to get you!" That's intercession. By a word of wisdom and word of knowledge, I can know what is going on in a specific situation. It is not just prayer; it is a whole attitude of living that we can have where we want to walk by the Spirit so that we know how to help people in a time of need. This way we can give them the encouragement they need. If it is a warning that danger is approaching, by revelation we can tell them to take a specific action.

A simple definition of intercession is to meet with God to entreat or ask him for something specific for a person. It could be for yourself as well. The simple picture is to meet. It is meeting with God because we intercede to God. We pray to God so we meet with God to entreat him for something specific.

About ten years ago I learned a wonderful truth when praying and interceding for a baby who was really sick. It was a desperate situation and God showed me that I needed to turn away from looking at the circumstances and only look to him for the deliverance for the child. This principle has helped me in many times of ministering since, where even the other day, I knew that I could not look at the actual reality of things going on when praying for someone. There have been many answers to prayer and victories by doing this. Sometimes, especially when someone is close to us, it is more difficult to do this. But God is the greatest authority and also the Shepherd. He knows how to take care of his children in the best possible way. That is what we can trust and rely on.

Jeremiah was an incredible prayer warrior and intercessor. He prophesied for more than forty years, pleading with Judah to try to get them to understand how to come back to God. They rarely listened to him, except to try to prove him wrong.

> Jeremiah 27:14-18 ESV
> 14 Do not listen to the words of the prophets who are saying to you, 'You shall not serve the king of Babylon,' for it is a lie that they are prophesying to you.
> 15 I have not sent them, declares the LORD, but they are prophesying falsely in my name, with the result that I will drive you out and you will perish, you and the prophets who are prophesying to you.
> 16 Then I spoke to the priests and to all this people, saying, "Thus says the LORD: Do not listen to the words of your prophets who are prophesying to you, saying, 'Behold, the vessels of the LORD's house will now shortly be brought back from Babylon' for it is a lie that they are prophesying to you.
> 17 Do not listen to them; serve the king of Babylon and live. Why should this city become a desolation?
> 18 If they are prophets, and if the word of the LORD is with them, then let them intercede with the LORD of hosts, that the vessels that are left in the house of the LORD, in the house of the king of Judah, and in Jerusalem may not go to Babylon.

In verse 18, Jeremiah is actually talking to some priests who listened to false prophets. This verse exemplifies moving in between a situation and God to get his solution. God had prophesied that the vessels from the temple were going to go to Babylon. That was the prophesy from Jeremiah and from the true God. The other prophets were saying that it wasn't true, "Oh no no no, it doesn't have to be like that. They're not going to have to go to Babylon; we'll rescue them from out of there." Basically, they were being very prideful in believing that they would be the intercessors. Jeremiah called them on it by saying that if they were really prophets then they would entreat God that something would happen so the vessels would not go to Babylon. That is intercession. When you know something detrimental is going to happen, then it's not just praying against it. It is specifically moving in between to ask him what to do to prevent something from happening. When something evil is already moving, it is stepping in between to stop it.

Now that we have seen the two basic kinds of prayer, let's look at how to make prayer a lifestyle.

PRAYER IS A CRY FROM THE HEART

> *Psalm 5:1-3 ESV*
> *1 Give ear to my words, O LORD; consider my groaning.*
> *2 Give attention to the sound of my cry, my King and my God, for to you do I pray.*
> *3 O LORD, in the morning you hear my voice; in the morning I prepare a sacrifice for you and watch.*

Prayer also requires listening and watching. It is not just our crying out to God, but listening for his "still, small voice" in return.

PRAYER IS A CONVERSATION

When Moses was on the mountain getting the two tablets, he came down to see the children of Israel worshipping a golden calf. He then spent 40 days and nights in prayer and intercession for the people. This is part of his conversation with God. It says that Moses spoke with God "face to face" (Deuteronomy 34:10). You can read the rest of the record about how God answered this prayer.

> *Deuteronomy 9:25-27 ESV*
> *25 So I lay prostrate before the LORD for these forty days and forty nights, because the LORD had said he would destroy you.*
> *26 And I prayed to the LORD, "O Lord GOD, do not destroy your people and your heritage, whom you have redeemed through your greatness, whom you have brought out of Egypt with a mighty hand.*

27 Remember your servants, Abraham, Isaac, and Jacob. Do not regard the stubbornness of this people, or their wickedness or their sin,

PRAYER IS PETITION FOR SOMETHING SPECIFIC

Matthew 7:7-11 APNT
7 Ask and it will be given to you. Seek and you will find. Knock and it will be opened to you.
8 For everyone who asks will receive and he who seeks will find and to him who knocks, it will be opened to him.
9 Or what man among you, whose son asks him for bread, will hold out a stone to him?
10 And if he asks him for a fish, will he hold out a snake to him?
11 And if therefore you who are evil know to give good gifts to your sons, how much more will your Father who is in heaven give good [gifts] to those who ask him?

In this passage, the asking, seeking and knocking is a continuous action until we see the "good gifts" given to those who ask.

PRAYER CHANGES THINGS AND INTERRUPTS SATAN'S PLANS

Acts 4:24-31 APNT
24 And when they heard [it], they raised their voice as one to God and said, "LORD, you are God, who made the heaven and earth and seas and everything that is in them.
25 And it is you who spoke by way of the Holy Spirit by the mouth of David your servant: Why do the nations rage and the people consider vanity?
26 The kings of the earth and the rulers have risen up and have deliberated as one against the Lord and against his Messiah.
27 For truly Herod and Pilate with the Gentiles and the congregation of Israel were gathered together in this city against the Holy [one], your Son, Jesus, whom you anointed,

28 to do everything that your hand and your will foreordained to be [done].

29 And also now, LORD, look and see their threats and allow your servants to boldly preach your word,

30 while you extend your hand for healings and mighty works and signs to be [done] in the name of your holy Son, Jesus."

31 And after they had prayed and made [this] request, the place in which they were gathered was shaken and all of them were filled with the Holy Spirit and were boldly speaking the word of God.

Prayer changes the outcomes of things in our lives. That is why we can learn to continue to "seek the shepherding of the strong one" and "speak to the greatest authority" and find out his answers to the situations in our own lives as well as for others. We can walk in victory each day by learning to "pray without ceasing" (1 Thessalonians 5:17). God even helps us with knowing what to pray for.

Romans 8:26-31 APNT

26 So also, the Spirit aids our weakness, for we do not know what is right to pray for. But the Spirit prays on our behalf with groans that are not describable.

27 Now he who searches the hearts knows what is the thinking of the Spirit that prays on behalf of the holy [ones] according to the will of God.

28 But we know that those who love God, he aids in everything for good, those whom he determined beforehand to be called [ones].

29 And from the first he knew them and marked them out with the likeness of the image of his Son, that he would be the firstborn of many brothers.

30 And those whom he marked out beforehand, he called, and those whom he called, he justified, and those whom he justified, he glorified.

31 What then should we say about these [things]? If God [is] for us, who is against us?

Chapter 20 ❖ Praise in Everything

The Psalms is called the book of praises, *sepher tehillim. Tehillim* is defined as "all that is worthy of praise and celebration." What is worthy of praise? The answer is the pervading theme of the Psalms – the works and ways of the Lord (Jehovah).

The Psalms show how God brings deliverance, peace, joy, health and protection to his people. It is invariably the expression of the magnitude and depth of God working with his people. The thematic content of the Psalms is in essence, personal. It is an "I–thee" relationship where the believer is describing, imploring, worshipping, magnifying God. The "I" may mean an individual or apply to a whole congregation. It is still basically an individual expression. This personal content means that the psalm is written out of a particular believer's heart and life. It may come as a result of an historical event or situation or out of a moment of enlightened understanding. In either case, it comes from the heart of man to his God and Lord.

> *Deuteronomy 10:21 NASB*
> *He is your praise [tehillah] and He is your God, who has done these great and awesome things for you which your eyes have seen.*

As the final chapter in this book on exploring practical keys about our journey of life, I think it is appropriate to briefly look at how praise can be in everything we do, just like prayer. In fact, the two are uniquely entwined together.

The two main words translated praise in Hebrew are *yadah* and *halal. Yadah* means "to confess," literally "to stretch out the hand." The first use in the Bible is in Genesis 29:35. Leah's fourth child was named Judah, which means "praise the Lord." The first use of *yadah* in Psalms gives more insight into the depth of the word.

Chapter 20 ∴ Praise in Everything

Psalm 7:17 KJV
I will praise [yadah] the Lord according to his righteousness: and will
sing praise to the name of the Lord most high.

The standard of what to confess or praise is according to God's righteousness. Whenever *yadah* is used, it is in reference to what God has done, either in mighty works or for an individual. It is a description of what God has done. In this sense it comes out of specific situations and is the confession of an individual's heart of what God has done for them. An example of this kind of praise is in Psalm 18. The Lord is called a rock, a fortress or mountain stronghold, a deliverer, a high tower. It is the confession of David of what God did for him and who God was to him. God is described as "my strength, in whom I will trust."

This confession or praise, *yadah*, becomes vividly understood because it is linked with thanksgiving. It is translated 37 times in the King James Version as thank or give thanks.

Psalm 18:49-50 NASB
49 Therefore I will give thanks [yadah] to Thee among the nations, O
LORD, And I will sing praises to Thy name.
50 He gives great deliverance to His king, And shows lovingkindness to
His anointed, To David and his descendants forever.

The second main word for praise is *halal* and this word incorporates the idea of celebration and rejoicing. The transliteration into English is hallelujah. It is to praise the Lord with an exclamation point! The use of this word often has to do with God's mighty works of creation, his greatness and omnipotence. There are five psalms called the Hallelujah Psalms, 146-150, which begin and end with "praise the Lord."

These two kinds of praise describe the gamut of expression in the Psalms. They were used together in the temple worship services. Here is an example of one place where the two words are used. We can see that thanksgiving is to confess and tell of all God's wonderful works.

> *1 Chronicles 16:7-12 ESV*
> *7 Then on that day David first appointed that thanksgiving [yadah] be sung to the LORD by Asaph and his brothers.*
> *8 Oh give thanks [yadah] to the LORD; call upon his name; make known his deeds among the peoples!*
> *9 Sing to him, sing praises [zamar] to him; tell of all his wondrous works!*
> *10 Glory [halal] in his holy name; let the hearts of those who seek the LORD rejoice!*
> *11 Seek the LORD and his strength; seek his presence continually!*
> *12 Remember the wondrous works that he has done, his miracles and the judgments he uttered,*

There is another word translated praise, but it is used together with singing. This word *zamar* is translated to sing praises, to sing psalms. It is not used separately from *yadah* or *halal* and covers both aspects praise. Thus, to sing praises is to put both confession and celebration into music.

> *Psalm 108:1-5 ESV*
> *1 My heart is steadfast, O God! I will sing and make melody with all my being!*
> *2 Awake, O harp and lyre! I will awake the dawn!*
> *3 I will give thanks [yadah] to you, O LORD, among the peoples; I will sing praises [zamar] to you among the nations.*
> *4 For your steadfast love is great above the heavens; your faithfulness reaches to the clouds.*
> *5 Be exalted, O God, above the heavens! Let your glory be over all the earth!*

Chapter 20 ∴ Praise in Everything

The overall theme of the Psalms is this personal expression of praise to our Lord and God. The purpose of praise is to glorify God and magnify his deliverance and love for His people. We can praise (confess and thank) and rejoice (celebrate) for all God, our Jehovah Elohim, has done for us and have the same kind of temple worship they had in the Old Testament in our day-by-day lives.

> *2 Chronicles 5:13 KJV*
> *It came even to pass, as the trumpeters and singers were as one, to make one sound to be heard in praising, [halal] and thanking [yadah] the Lord; and when they lifted up their voice with the trumpets and cymbals and instrument of musick, and praised [halal] the Lord, saying, For he is good; for his mercy endureth for ever: that then the house was filled with a cloud, even the house of the Lord.*

There are other words in both Hebrew and Greek that mean praise of one form or another, everything from quiet kneeling or bowing down to God to shouting, crying and dancing. But no matter what form the praise takes, it is basically either thanks or celebration.

In the New Testament and considering our walk in Christ, we have even more to be thankful for and to celebrate. We can also praise God by speaking in tongues and singing spiritual songs. As we do this, then praise becomes something we do all the time, not just in a worship service. We are to give thanks and do everything in the name of our Lord Jesus Christ.

> *Colossians 3:14-17 APNT*
> *14 And with all these [things], [put on] love, which is the girdle of maturity.*
> *15 And the peace of Christ will govern your hearts, for to him you were called in one body. And be thankful to Christ,*

Chapter 20 ∴ Praise in Everything

16 that his word may live in you richly with all wisdom. And teach and instruct yourselves in psalms and in hymns and in songs of the Spirit and sing with grace in your hearts to God.
17 And everything that you do in word and in work, do in the name of our Lord Jesus Christ and give thanks by way of him to God the Father.

CONCLUSION

I want to end this book with one of my favorite verses. It is powerful in both Greek and Aramaic.

> *Hebrews 13:5-6 APNT*
> *5 Your mind should not love money, but what you have should be sufficient for you. For the LORD has said: "I will not leave you and I will not let go of you."*
> *6 And we can say confidently: "My Lord is my helper. I will not be afraid. What does a man do to me?"*

The last part of verse 5 is quoted from Deuteronomy.

> *Deuteronomy 31:6 ESV*
> *Be strong and courageous. Do not fear or be in dread of them, for it is the LORD your God who goes with you. He will not leave you or forsake you.*

Consider the last phrase in this verse about not leaving you or forsaking you. According to Adam Clarke's Commentary, this verse is peculiarly emphatic in Greek.

> There are no less than five negatives in this short sentence, and these connected with two verbs and one pronoun twice repeated. To give a literal translation is scarcely possible; it would run in this way: "No, I will not leave thee; no, neither will I not utterly forsake thee." Those who understand the

135

genius of the Greek language, and look at the manner in which these negatives are placed in the sentence, will perceive at once how much the meaning is strengthened by them, and to what an emphatic and energetic affirmative they amount[26]

We could write that in English and it would say, "I will never, never, never, never, NEVER leave you." What an exhortation! What a promise from our great God!

The Aramaic translation is literally, "I will not leave you and my hands will not relax hold of you." God's hands will never hang down and do nothing. He is always working on our behalf and will never let go of our hands. That is why we can boldly say "the Lord is my helper" and not be afraid of anything.

As we walk this journey of life with our wonderful Father, our Lord and each other, let us remember that we are not alone. And let us continue to shine as lights in this crooked world with the sweet message of the gospel of peace.

> *2 Corinthians 2:14 APNT*
> *Now thanks be to God who always brings to pass triumph for us in Christ and by us makes evident the fragrance of the knowledge of him in every place.*

There are so many more topics that could be covered about our walk in Christ! Let me conclude the book with the principle that I have used to endeavor to explain aspects about our walk.

> *Psalm 119:105 NLT*
> *Your word is a lamp to guide my feet and a light for my path.*

---

[26] Adam Clarke, *Commentary on the Whole Bible*, E-Sword, Hebrew 13:5.

Chapter 20 ∴ Praise in Everything

With both the word of God and its instruction and the Spirit of Christ within, we can walk in balance and walk worthy of our calling. The word of God shows us what to do and how to do it and the Spirit gives us the specific information that we need to be able to walk in the good works "which God prepared beforehand, that we should walk in them" (Ephesians 2:10).

> *1 Corinthians 16:13-14 APNT*
> *13 Watch and stand in the faith. Act mature. Be strong.*
> *14 And all your affairs should be [done] with love.*

As we have explored keys to our practical walk in Christ, I trust that you have been encouraged to grow up into all we have been given so bountifully by our loving Father. Let's continue to live by faith and have our lives exemplify the maturity of the love of God in action.

Bibliography

SELECTED RESOURCES:

Hamilton, Adam. *The Walk*. Nashville, Tennessee: Abingdon Press, 2019.

Hartlaub, Steve. *Give Me Christ*. Steve Hartlaub, 2016.

Nee, Watchman. *Sit, Walk, Stand*. Carol Stream, Illinois: Tyndale House Publishers, 1977.

Paxson, Ruth. *The Wealth, Walk and Warfare of the Christian*. Westwood, New Jersey: Fleming H. Revell Company, 1936.

Wadge, Rik B. *Discovering the Jewish Roots of the Letter to the Ephesians*. Jewish Roots Publishing, 2015.

Welch, Charles H. *In Heavenly Places*. London: The Berean Publishing Trust, 1968.

REFERENCES AND DICTIONARIES:

Benner, Jeff. *The Ancient Hebrew Lexicon of the Bible*. College Station, Texas: Virtualbookworm.com, 2005.

Bullinger, E. W. *A Critical Lexicon and Concordance to the English and Greek New Testament*. Grand Rapids, Michigan: Zondervan Publishing House, 1975.

Girdlestone, Robert Baker. *Synonyms of the Old Testament*. Grand Rapids, Michigan: William B. Eerdmans Publishing, 1897 reprint.

Harris, R. Laird, Gleason L. Archer, Jr., Bruce K. Waltke, eds. *Theological Wordbook of the Old Testament*. 2 vols. Chicago: Moody Press, 1980.

Jennings, William. *Lexicon to the Syriac New Testament*. London: Oxford University Press, 1926.

Ryken, Leland, ed. *Dictionary of Biblical Imagery*. Downers Grove, Illinois: Inter-Varsity Press, 1998.

Smith, J. Payne. *A Compendious Syriac Dictionary*. London: Oxford at the Clarendon Press, 1967.

Bibliography

Thayer, Joseph Henry. *The New Thayer's Greek-English Lexicon of the New Testament.* Christian Copyrights, Inc., 1981.

Vine, W.E. *Vine's Expository Dictionary of Old and New Testament Words.* Old Tappan, New Jersey: Fleming H. Revell Company, 1981.

About the Author

Janet Magiera is an ordained minister and the founder of Light of the Word Ministry, a ministry dedicated to teaching and making known the understanding of the Aramaic language, figures of speech and customs of the Bible. In 1979, under the tutelage of a student of Dr. George M. Lamsa, Jan began pursuing a course of study of the Aramaic Peshitta New Testament. For over 40 years, she has taught in Bible fellowships and churches in the United States and other countries, using insight from her understanding of the biblical languages. Many articles and teachings of interest are available on the Light of the Word Ministry website, www.lightofword.org.

Jan began compiling a database of the Aramaic Peshitta New Testament in the early 1990's. As computer technology increased over the years, she expanded and developed the database to generate a series of research tools to study the New Testament. The entire database originally was developed as a software module for BibleWorks, which is no longer available for purchase. The database can now be searched online at www.aramaicdb.lightofword.org. In 2006, *The Aramaic Peshitta New Testament Translation* was published as the first book of a complete Aramaic Peshitta New Testament Library. The library includes an interlinear, lexicon, concordance and parallel translations. There is an app of the Aramaic translation on both Apple and Google, and there are various electronic versions of her books.

Jan has also authored several other topical books on biblical subjects: *Members in Particular* on the body of Christ, *The Armor of Victory* on the armor of God, *The Fence of Salvation* on Hebrew and Aramaic word pictures, *The Coming of the Son of Man* about the sequence of events of the end times and a study workbook for individuals and small groups called *Ephesians: Our Spiritual Treasure*. She has also released a revision of her book, *Enriched in Everything, Biblical Lessons on Giving*.

She and her husband Glen currently live in San Diego, California. Together they have four children and eleven grandchildren.

www.ingramcontent.com/pod-product-compliance
Lightning Source LLC
Chambersburg PA
CBHW072154090426
42740CB00012B/2258